Joscelyne's
of Old Leigh and

CW00498447

REVIEWS OF *Joscelyne's Beach*:

"Beyond the bounds of this idyllic place, two world wars came and went, generations grew and faded, and Southend relentlessly enlarged . . . This small patch of private foreshore somehow seemed to enshrine so much of Southend's – and the English seaside's history, as well as a haunting sense of a vanished happy world . . . If this book is as widely read as predicted, this bewitched morsel of land will once again become Joscelyne's Beach in the minds of people far beyond Essex."

The Evening Echo

"Here are recollections at first hand from Edwardian childhood to the 1940s, with a broad variety of people and events, hopes and disappointments brought to life with insight . . . Francis Turnidge the sailmaker; the magnificently uniformed Gravesend coastguards; a champagne-quaffing countess and many others. Boats are an underlying thread: a 'white elephant' hire dinghy too posh to use; a rowboat from Gamages which proved invaluable; buying a Gravesend shrimper for £20 . . . An unusual and beguiling book, with its background of sun, sand and seaweed."

Classic Boat

"This lyrical memoir offers a vivid insight into Leigh-on-Sea and its characters before, during and after the First World War."

Essex Magazine

JOSCELYNE'S TALES

OF OLD LEIGH AND CHALKWELL

Arthur Joscelyne

DESERT ISLAND BOOKS

First published in 2005
by
DESERT ISLAND BOOKS LIMITED
7 Clarence Road, Southend on Sea, Essex SS1 1AN
United Kingdom
www.desertislandbooks.com

British Library Cataloguing-in-Publication Data
A catalogue record for this book is available from the British Library

ISBN 1-874287-97-X

Printed in Great Britain
by 4Edge Ltd

Front cover illustration shows the framed water-colour which opens the
first story "The Great Race". It is still in the family's possession and is
inscribed "Dad's boat, hanging on the wall in Aunt Polly's front room".
It depicts Arthur's father in the boat which he raced from Rochester
down the Medway and across the Thames to Leigh around 1886.

Rear cover photograph shows the author, Arthur Joscelyne, then aged
about eighteen, on the "Wake Early" off Chalkwell beach.

Joscelyne's Beach extended for 200 yards on the north shore of the
River Thames and adjoined what became Chalkwell station on the
Southend Central to London Fenchurch Street railway line.

Author's Note & Contents

To those who have read my first book – SEAWEED, SAND & SALTWATER [a.k.a. *Joscelyne's Beach*], – any queries that might arise, and the general background of the short stories that follow, are self-explanatory. It is purely for convenience that I have separated, what is in reality, part of my earlier efforts to record some of the characters I met and so well remember, along the Leigh and Chalkwell Foreshore. But they can be read equally well either separately or together.

ARTHUR W. JOSCELYNE
(aged 79)
1982

Publisher's Note

When Clare Harvey brought me her late father, Arthur Joscelyne's, manuscript – SEAWEED, SAND & SALTWATER – it was clear she had in her possession one of the finest memoirs of Old Leigh and the Thames estuary ever recorded. We published it in 2004 under the title *Joscelyne's Beach*, and the first printing was quickly exhausted.

It is easy to explain the book's allure. Joscelyne, born in 1903, had spent his early manhood in the service of the family beach – 200 yards of foreshore by what is now Chalkwell railway station – leased from 1909 until after the Second World War. Joscelyne was in his eightieth year when he set himself to record his, and his family's history of "the Beach". Few other accounts of English coastal life, before, during and after the First World War, can match it for detail, insight and originality. The sea in all its guises comes alive in his hands, as do its creatures, human and otherwise.

Joscelyne, who died in 1993, bequeathed not just one book, but a small archive, none of it published in his lifetime. Whilst editing *Joscelyne's Beach* I pondered how to handle references to episodes followed up elsewhere, not included in the original text for fear of embarrassing those named. To ease readers' confusion, I deleted most of these references so that the book might stand intact.

Now those gaps can be filled. Joscelyne's second volume – SEE YER TER-MORRER, AND OTHER SHORT STORIES OF OLD LEIGH AND CHALKWELL – had been written in tandem with the first. It, too, was presented to me in hard binding, with fifteen tales folded and glued in place. A sixteenth – The "Old Wreck" – was attached separately and appears to have been included as an afterthought. It is no less precious for that, for it shows Joscelyne as a natural story teller, and is sure to send historians on the scent of the wreck.

Clare Harvey allowed me to rename SEE YER TER-MORRER as *Joscelyne's Tales*. It is not a sequel to *Joscelyne's Beach*, rather a companion to it. The time-scale is the same, flesh is put on personalities lightly sketched or overlooked in *Joscelyne's Beach*, and the world of Leigh-on-Sea and its larger-than-life characters from nearly a century ago comes vividly to life.

CLIVE LEATHERDALE
Desert Island Books

1

The Great Race

On Auntie Polly's front room wall there hung a small, black-framed water colour of a small sailing boat, a helmsman and two others sitting in the stern and, in the background, another identical craft. Not a work of art but the hallmarks of a sincere artist and inscribed in tiny letters in one corner "E.P.R. 15/7[18]86". Only on rare occasions did I enter this holy of holies but chance did cause me to be invited in (to hang some curtains) and for the first time I became sufficiently interested to inspect it closely and ask about it. (It now hangs on my wall.)

"That was Arthur's – your Dad's – boat," was Auntie's reply.

"That's not the 'green boat'," I said.

"No, it's the one he had when he was a young man, long before you were thought of. And many's the good sail I had with him in her." Then she added as an afterthought, "when he wasn't racing with that Reuben Williams and his boat at the back. An artist friend who used to stay with us painted it for me and you shall have it when I'm gone."

So the first seeds of interest were sown and I determined to find if possible a little more about Dad's boat. On my frequent visits as a child to the Old Town, Dad would often stop and chat or call in at The Smack for a pint with Reuben. I knew he was still around, although now a very old man, and I knew his haunts; they hadn't varied since those early days. And sure enough, I found him seated on a bench overlooking Bell Wharf, his usual seat until opening time.

I went up to him. "You're Reuben, aren't you?" He peered at me with aging eyes.

"I don't rightly recollect who you be," he said.

"I'm Arthur Joscelyne's boy," I replied.

He looked me over. "You ain't much like him, he were short an' dark if my memory serves me, aye, and as artful as a wagon load o' monkeys as I remembers well. Bin gone this many a year."

"Do you remember my Auntie Polly?" was my next question.

"Aye, that I do. She was a fine gal, a bit sharpish of tongue, kept yer Dad in his place," and almost to himself I heard him mutter, "the only one as could." A distant light came into his old eyes; I could see he was back in the Old Leigh of yesteryear and I thought, "Now's the time to ask him about Dad's boat and how much he remembers of it."

"Remember it? O' course I do, like as if it was yes'day."

"Tell me about it," I said.

"It's a long story," he replied and with careful precision produced a large silver watch from his pocket, consulted it and remarked that, "Story telling makes me throat that dry as yer never would believe," and anyway, it was nigh time he was getting away. I told him I would take care of his dry throat and there was still a half an hour to opening time, long enough I thought for my purpose.

"Well, it's a long story," he repeated, "which bit might you want to hear?"

"As much as you can tell me. Why not start at the beginning," I said.

"Aye, I s'pect that's as good as anywhere, so sit yerself comf'table an' I'll tell ee.

"It all started when yer Dad and me was having a pint tergether in The Ship and this 'ere notice stuck up about an "ockshun" [auction] at Chatham Docks on the Sat'day a following. All sorts of gear as 'oud please a sailor man, anchors, chains, blocks and sichlike and some ship's boats what interested yer Dad an' me. So we arranged with Bill Emery to sail us up to Rochester on the Friday in his bawley. We stopped the night in a little pub by the river so as to be nice an' arly at the ockshun on the next day, so as to have a good look at what was a going. And among 'em was half a dozen small "whalers" alike as peas in a pod, so much so that only their numbers what was cut in their starn was dif'rent. Yer Dad and me agreed to wait an' see how the prices was going and not bid agin each other as any one on 'em was as good as t'other. And the upshot was we buys one each for five pun a time.

"Each on 'em had its gear and sichlike and a mast an' leg o' mutton sail." [A "leg o' mutton sail" was a loose footed sail on a gaff and fastened in the front by a shackle to the stem head, making it like a combined foresail and mainsail and much the shape of

8

a "leg of mutton".) "There was no sense in hanging around, so we gets some sailors to help us launch 'em, ups the sails an' sets off 'ome on the fallin' tide. "Race yer home," sez yer Dad. "Bottle of gin for the winner." "Done," says I and off we goes.

"Well, they two boats might well have bin tied tergether. There was a fairish breeze blowing down river and we was a stone's throw away from each other when we gits to Sheerness. We could 'ave shook hands when we reached the end of the boom and started across the river to 'ome. We made it down the swatch and crossed the tail end of the middle sand and when we gits to the Low Way he weren't but a rope's length behind me, me having nipped his wind as being to wind'ard of 'im. It were a 'ard punch up the Low Way an' into the Ray, the tide being what it was and the banks a-showin'. But we gits up Leigh Crick as far as we can, anchors them an' calls it a draw, to be fought out fair an' square the Sat'day following, the winner to 'ev his bottle of gin, like afore.

"Well, the tale gits around among the Leighmen an' even them as is t'other side of the pier, and it weren't that long afore they was placing their bets on one or t'other of us. When Sat'day comes there's a half tidy crowd of locals and fisherfolk to watch us all lined up like it was a "regatter" [regatta]. The course was to the Low Way buoy round the "Chapman light" starting and ending at Bell Wharf.

"It were blowing fairish from the sou'-west, just the right wind for both of us. We started across the line tergether and we comes back tergether and if it hadn't a bin a row boat full of kids what got in me way I'd hev beat yer Dad. I'm not so certain sure as how them kids wasn't there a purpose to stop me with all that betting money an' all.

Well, yer Dad gits his bottle of gin, an' I gives 'im 'is due, he shared it with me and our mates in The Ship. Them as won their bets did us proud an' said as how I should hev won, them kids not being there, and it would be only fair if we did it all over agin in a fortnight when the tides come round agin, to prove it. Well the word gits around, and the landlord of The Ship puts up a small barrel of best fourpenny ale for the winner, and him to collect and hold the bets, a half tidy bit too from what I 'ears.

"So when the time comes round we did the race all over agin and this time I winned fair and square. But there was only a boat's

9

length betwix us 'cause them two boats being built so much alike was same as twins who couldn't abide being apart one from t'other. Like I said, I beat him fair an' square but I hit the marking buoy and they said it had to be done agin, but I gets the fust prize jist the same. And so it went on all through that year, sometimes yer Dad beat me, sometimes I beat him. All the time the prizes an' bets and folks as come to see was gitting bigger and bigger 'cause we both made sure only to beat each other by a little bit. It was my idea to keep the ball a rollin', now it was coming a sort of reg'lar supply of beer and sichlike an' the race kind of gitting famous, as yer can rightly understand.

"When 'regatter' time comes round we was put as a separate event down on the list. It was my notion, as more come to see us than see "Gotty" walk the greasy pole, which 'e allus won, owing, some do say, to 'im having long toes like monkeys hev. But to my mind it's 'cause he allus waits till last, when most of the grease be wiped off, if yer sees me meaning."

Here he stopped, once again searched for his watch, carefully inspected the time and started to rise. In a panic I said, " But you're just coming to the most interesting part."

"Maybe," he said, "but it can wait an' me thirst won't. I allus gits thirsty when folks get me talking a lot, so I'll bid yer good day." I took the hint.

"Wait a moment." I put my hand in my pocket and found a half crown. "Have a pint on me, will you?" He spat on it, put it in his pocket, winked one wicked old eye and shambled off up the cobblestone High Street. Suddenly he turned.

"See yer termorrer," he called out and then continued on his way.

I think it was that wink that did it. I had a vague but ever-increasing suspicion that it was not entirely chance that had interrupted his story at its most interesting and exciting point. I dearly wanted to hear how it finished.

Next day found me early at his usual seat and I waited impatiently for his arrival, but strangely enough, it was only a half hour to opening time before he hove in sight and sat down beside me.

"I've bin kept," he said as he mopped his face with a large red and white spotted handkerchief, although there seemed little need for it, or any signs of hurry on his countenance. "Yus, I've bin kept," he repeated, and launched off with a long – or it would have been long – story of the misdemeanours of his son-in-law who, it seemed, lived with him. At any other time I would have loved to listen to it but I had a strange feeling he was deliberately stalling for time, so I impatiently interrupted.

"What happened about the race you were telling me all about yesterday?"

"Oh that," he said, and I thought for a moment he was going to dismiss it offhand and go on with his son-in-law's failings. Then realizing there was little future in it, he said, "How for did I git?"

"Coming up to the Leigh regatta," I replied.

I knew I had won; the distant look came back in his eyes, searching the past, and my hopes arose. He chuckled deep down in his beard. "Yus, he allus won a little pig."

I interrupted. "How did Dad win a pig?"

"Not yer Dad," he said impatiently. "Gotty."

I said, "What's Gotty and a pig got to do with it?"

"Well, like I was a sayin', Gotty allus won, and the fust prize was a little pig as was put in a box at the end of the bawley's bowsprit, what was all covered in thick grease, and the fust 'un as got to the box an' got the pig winned it for 'iself."

I turned this bit of information over in my mind. "Ah," I said, "But how did he get that pig back along that greasy pole to the bawley?"

"He didn't," said Reuben. "When he got to 'im, he opens the box and chucks 'im in the water, where like as not he'd make for the shore while Gotty jumped in arter 'im to help 'im on his way. But mos' times it never got there alive, cos pigs can swim, but they cuts their own throats with their sharp trotters in so doing. So yer hev to swim with 'em to get 'em ashore dead or alive so as to ock-shun 'em off to the highest bidder in the crowd when yer gits there. But them "animal kindness" people put a stop to it and now they gives yer the money in place o' the porker."

With that he stopped, fumbled in his pocket, consulted his watch, got to his feet and started on his way. "Time to git me 'med-icine'," he said, "but yer can walk along a' me to the shop."

"Good," I thought, "Perhaps I'll find out a bit more about the boat race on the way." But somehow the conversation seemed to revolve entirely around his "rheumatics" and the necessity of a half a bottle of gin, the only thing seemingly that kept him walkin'.

So up past the old station, across the level crossing and a little way up Leigh Hill we arrived at McKenzies, the off licence. He invited me to go in with him, selected the brand he favoured and dug into his pocket with some difficulty. Perhaps it was the rheumatics in his fingers that made it so difficult to find the money.

"Here, let me pay," I said in a reckless moment. His hands stopped searching almost at once.

"Since yer insist, I'm sure I'm much obliged." And once again that vague suspicion came to mind, and worse, I was no nearer to the end of the story. Outside again we went our separate ways but as he toddled off he called once more over his shoulder, "See yer termorrer."

As I climbed Leigh Hill I became more than ever convinced I was a victim of a clever old rascal, even at this moment planning how to keep up the fun of "having me on" and to enjoy the benefits accruing from it. I tried hard to think of a way to defeat his artfulness and yet hear the end of his story, and eventually came up with a plan I thought worth trying.

Next day he was even later arriving. There was only a quarter of an hour to opening time and, as I rather anticipated, he intended to fill that time probably with anything other than what I had come for, with perhaps sufficient reference to the story to whet my appetite, and so I would continue to contribute to slaking his thirst for some little time yet to come. I couldn't help but admire his ingenuity and the sense of artfulness and skill he possessed, and I am sure it was the fun he was having at my expense that pleased him much more than the fruits of it. But I had no intention of letting him get away with it indefinitely, besides which I couldn't spare the time to lose a morning for a quarter of an hour's talk.

He bid me good morning. "I've bin kept agin," he said, once again going through the performance of yesterday with his handkerchief to wipe non-existent sweat from his brow. "Yus, I'd hev bin 'ere early if I hadn't bin kept. It's that lazy b**ger of a son-in-law o' mine. Half the day in bed, t'other half sprawled right across in front of the fire and me what has to chop the wood an' light it and buy the coal and keep it a going. Comes to summat when yer can't sit in front o' yer own fire. I sez to 'im, 'git off yer backside for one'st and let me see the colour of the fire.' When I pulls the chair from under 'im he calls me an old bastard, what I never was. I minded 'im of 'is mother's sister as had a couple of kids and no husband and slammed the door an' left him to chew that one over.'

I could see I wasn't going to get far again today. His hand went to his pocket and he produced his watch. "Gittin' nigh time I wus going. Care to walk along o' me as far as The Ship?" he asked hopefully. "All this upsetting and talking allus makes me throat dry."

It was then I produced my trump card – or at least I hoped it was. "Well, we'll cure that straight away," and picking up the bag I had brought with me, I produced a large bottle of ale and a glass, filled it and passed it to him. He drank it down, wiped his lips and said, "Ain't yer going to hev one?"

"No," I said, "I don't care for beer. The rest is yours, and there's enough left to stop you getting thirsty until you tell me the rest of what happened when you and Dad raced. You've had your bit of fun, but I want to hear how it finished."

I think he realized I was up to his little tricks. A smile wreathed his old face. "Yer ain't much like yer Dad to look at but you've got his ways, an' if yer don't much mind I'll hev another glass an' then I'll tell ee the rest o' it. How far did I git?" He slowly finished his glass. I picked up the bottle.

"The rest will be nice when you've finished," I said and put it back in the bag and added, "You got to where you and Dad were put down as a special entry in the regatta."

"Aye, that was it," he said. "I knowed, yer didn't 'ave to tell me. Well, when the word gits around, the landlord of The Ship puts up an extra ten pun, that's on top of the prize money of a fiver, and you never did see sich betting as went on. And him as I don't hold with, as got The Smack, promised a barrel o' beer. Yer Dad's people at The Bell puts up a bottle of gin an' a bottle of whiskey an' this time yer Dad and me promised we'd settle it once an' for all, except for a bit of fun now and agin like.

"The day afore the regatter I 'eard yer father had got his boat up along where Francy Tonnidge's [Francis Turnidge's] shop is an' was a black-leading her bottom and a polishing of it like as if it was his best shoes, to make her go faster. So me and my mate Charley gits ours up by the Smack launch and cleans and scrubs and black-leads same as yer Dad, and Charley does one or two lit-tle other jobs jist in case." He stopped and chuckled to himself.

"Just in case of what?" I said.

With a grin he said, "Niver yer mind. P'raps I tell yer an' p'raps I won't."

His old eyes took that far away look. "It were a lovely day that regatter an' folks come from all around and even from Lunnon so I wus told. Certain they came from Wak'ring, Shoebury, Rochford and Hadleigh, maybe arter Gotty's pig or maybe just to see 'em fall off the greasy pole, cos most of 'em didn't know one end of a boat from t'other, except them as had their betting money on me and yer Dad. There weren't not a breath of wind when we lined up on the startin' line. The course was from Bell Wharf, round a bawley wiv a flag on it at the far end o' the bay, round the Old Watch Boat and back to Bell Wharf. But owing to there being no wind to speak of, it was now jist to the bawley an' back, we was told.

"I had me mate Charley with me but yer Dad was on 'is own, said as how he didn't want no extra weight. I gets right out to wind'ard of him by the startin' buoy an' he kept inshore to miss the tide. But the tide still took him back but we seemed to find the breeze cos we got over the line and ketched a cap full a' wind, or so it seemed to yer Dad, and soon arter we was twenty lengths or more ahead of 'im.

"Then a puff of air comes across the water and we both gets a little way. Sometimes we gets a breeze of wind, sometimes we don't. It took two hours to git there an' back but we beat yer Dad by a hundred yards and winned fust prize easy an' all t'other prizes as well. Yer Dad was hopping mad and he never knowed how we done it, nor yet anyone else for that matter, except me mate Charley and he's gone now. Wouldn't hev done, what wiv all them prizes and bets and sichlike a hanging on it."

"And how *did* you do it?" I enquired, sensing another added interest to his story.

"Aye, that's telling," he said. His hand went to his watch pock-et. "Time's a getting on," and he eased himself onto his legs.

I thought, "He's caught me again. He's going to get away with 'until termorrer', but I'll have one last try," and picking up the bag and bottle that lay beside me, said, "Well, you might as well finish what's left in the bottle and finish the rest of the story at the same time."

The temptation was too much. He sat down again. I thought, "I've beaten the old rascal," and between sips he continued the rest of the story.

"Well as I wus a saying, when Charley and me brings her into the Smack slip to black her bottom, we done some other little jobs at the same time, jist in case.

"Just in case of what?" I asked again.

"Hold on a bit, I'm a comin' to that. Jist in case it was a flat calm, like it were, and like we thought it wus a going to be."

Deeply intrigued now with this new aspect, I could hardly wait for him to continue.

"Me mate Charley was pritty 'andy wiv 'is tools, by way of workin' for Tom Bundick the boat builder. When the rest of 'em, what was a watching but forgits to lend a hand in the scrubbing and blacking, went off into The Smack, he gits out his bag o' tools an' cuts half a dozen rivets out o' two of her planks jist below her gunwale amidships. Then he does two saw cuts down alongside her timbers and two bits of old seaboot leather for hinges, the whole lot makin' a nice little door, jist handy enough to git one of them basins on a handle what they calls 'ship's boilers' and yer arm through. When we rubbed a bit putty an' blacked it over in the cuts, her being black all over, a blind man 'oud a bin pleased to see it. Then Charley ups and gits a sack and stuffs it wi' shavings and puts one of his old "gernsies" and cap in it and stows it away in the back locker. And jist like we thought, when regatter day come the water's flatter not a board and no wind. We knowed we hadn't wasted our time and that's why we got well to wind'ard of yer Dad.

"Charley props his dressed up sack alongside me, 'cause only a little bit of it was showing and lays flat on the floorboards, opens his little door, sticks his arm and basin through and paddles as hard as he could. That's why we was a going for'ard while yer Dad was going back'ards, an' each time we sees our chance, down goes Charlie an' up comes the sack of straw to take 'is place and each time we gits further ahead of yer Dad and beats 'im. We put the sack back in the locker and the next day Charley mended them planks like there never wus no door an' we kept our mouths shut so as no one never knowed." He sighed, "It's long forgotten now

15

an' don't matter that much and as it consarns yer Dad, yer best know."

His hand went to his pocket; he consulted his watch. "Time I was a goin'." I helped him to his feet. "If yer sees yer Auntie Polly, remember me to 'er. If she hadn't bin so sharpish o' tongue I'd a courted her meself." His old eyes lighted up; a new thought struck him. "I might even have bin yer uncle then." I patted him affectionately on the back.

"I'm not so sure I'd want you as an uncle, you old rascal," I said with a smile.

"That's as maybe. But I still wishes as you was me nephew." I was flattered and delighted by this unexpected tribute, in fact so pleased I slipped half a crown into his hand.

"That will take care of tomorrow's thirst," I said. He didn't seem to notice.

"Cos if yer was me nephew then I wouldn't hev to go home to that lazy, good for nothin' son-in-law o' mine sprawled across the floor an' a shuttin' out the fire. And as for calling me out o' name, I got a paper what proves me Mum and Dad was wed all proper and above board." I could see present day problems had taken over from the past. We reached the level crossing. "Well, I'll bid yer good day," he said, "Likely I might see yer termorrer."

And as I watched his retreating figure, I rather wished I was, I'd grown that fond of the old rascal.

2

Findings, Keepings

The sun lay low on the horizon, and yet it was but two hours or so to midday. It gave a gentle warmth out of keeping with the time of year; a pale ghost of the previous summer, now many weeks gone, returning for a brief moment, to be finally exorcised by the coming winter.

And as I walked down Leigh Hill, past St. Clements, whose ivy covered tower stood sentinel over the tiled and slated cluster of roofs that comprised Old Leigh, I reached the Cliff Top. The river sparkled in the golden sunlight, divided by a patch of pure gold until lost in the remains of the earlier morning mist shrouding the Kent shore. And in its centre two or maybe three bawleys, with a halo of smoke floating over them as they stoked their coppers and cooked their catch of shrimps, stood out in sharp relief to their companions lined up in two orderly rows on either side, as though the Creator of all this beauty had selected them for special mention.

I had seen this scene so many times yet every time it was different, but never once had it left the impression on me that it did this morning. This was the Leigh of my ancestors. Of my father, his father, and many before him. They also had looked down on this ever changing panorama, and our footsteps had walked the same cobble stones of Old Leigh. I was proud that it was so.

Memories of those happy carefree days with Dad came flooding back and with them an overpowering urge to see and talk with that lovable old rascal, Reuben, for such I still thought him. He had made a deeper impression on me than I had first imagined and far from forgetting him, after our first encounter, he now figured more and more persistently in my thoughts. Maybe, I told myself, it was his close links with my father and the past, or more likely, perhaps I'd fallen for the artful charm that seemed so much part of his character. Whatever it was, it had become more and more insistent as time went by. And this lovely morning of all mornings found my footsteps leading, not as I intended, to the beach, but down the hill, past Uncle Fred's Blacksmiths Shop, now closed and deserted, over the bridge at the Bell Approach (no longer there) and to Bell Wharf.

I wasn't completely sure I wanted to see him. Possibly, if I just walked past and he wasn't there, this urge would die a quiet death and get out of my system. But fate had decreed otherwise. Obviously the fine morning that had brought me there had also persuaded him to do the same, and there he sat on his usual seat, but this time, not alone.

His companion was very old and very small, but by no means lacking in girth. He was dressed in jacket and trousers that had a distinct nautical touch. But he was most noticeable by the mass of white hair and beard that surrounded and almost buried two pale blue eyes, his pink cheeks and a short flat nose. Thick white hair clustered and framed too the underside of his wide brimmed, round, black hat (much like those worn by Catholic Priests) and I gained the general impression that he wasn't so much a human being as a dressed up sheep dog. And I say this in no unkindly way.

Reuben greeted me with genuine affection. There was no doubt by his manner he was pleased to see me and I, in turn, was delighted that I had given in to my desire to renew our previous acquaintance. We exchanged the usual greetings and Reuben, to show he wasn't entirely ignorant of the rules of etiquette, turned slightly towards his companion, and jabbing the air towards him with his finger, informed me, "This 'ere is Mr. 'Enery White. We calls 'im 'Snowball'. Mind yer, not so much on account of his name, as yer might rightly think, but cos 'is 'air 'as allus bin white, since he was a little 'un and from the day 'e was borned." And with that he bent towards the old man's ear and shouted, "Always 'ad white 'air since the day you was borned, ain't yer 'Enery?"

Then Reuben turned to me and said, "'E don't much like being called 'Snowball' to 'is face." A series of jerks and gestures acknowledged from within the hair that he was pleased to acknowledge being a person of some distinction, then he relapsed once again to the quiet tranquillity that I had disturbed.

Reuben then asked after Auntie Polly. Had I given her his kind regards? I hadn't, but to cover my lapse, told a few white lies which seemed to please him. I was about to probe his memory of further knowledge of Dad and Old Leigh when 'Enery suddenly became alive and tugged anxiously at Reuben's sleeve. A thin treble voice came through the hair and a quite unintelligible message passed between them. The old man cupped his hand to his ear and Reuben bent down again and shouted, "Arthur Jos-lin's boy, 'im as I used to race wiv." Seemingly quite satisfied the old man once again settled down with a few more nods and jerks of his head towards me.

"Wanted to know who yer was," said Reuben apologetically, "But it ain't no good a'telling on 'im, cos 'e never remembers. Most likely 'e'll ask me agin soon. 'E's as deaf as a post, but 'e won't 'ave it. Sez 'e's only 'ard o' 'earin, that' s all, but 'e don't talk much, which is all to the good, seeing as 'ow 'e's a-livin' along a-me now."

I turned this bit of information over in my mind.

"Makes it a bit crowded in front of your fire, doesn't it Reuben," I remarked with curiosity. "Especially with that son-in-law you were telling me about."

"Oh, 'im, I've got shot o' 'im. Me and me old mate," jerking a thumb at the now sleeping figure beside him, "share's it now, and *he* knows 'is place."

I scented a story. "Was it difficult?" I asked.

"Aye, I'll say it were, but it's too long to be a'telling of. I best be gitting along now." He consulted a large silver watch, struggled to his feet and prodded his companion into wakefulness. He helped him up and turned towards home with 'Enery trailing just behind.

Was he up to his old tricks? He hadn't mentioned being thirsty, but the old signs were there to see. If I wanted the story it was on his terms, not mine, and the fact I had shown interest hadn't escaped him. "See yer termorrer," he called, over his shoulder. I had little doubt now. But could I take that chance so late in the year. I might not have another fine day for months and it was certain he'd not be there if it wasn't. It was now or never.

"Hold on, Reuben," I shouted. "Wait for me". If it had to be The Ship, maybe I could buy the drinks and hear what he had to say in some quiet corner. It was all on the spur of the moment. I might even then just be wasting my time, but committed, I could do little else.

It transpired that 'Enery had to be taken home first, seated in his share of the fireplace to continue his interrupted slumber and, when he was comfortably settled, Reuben would slip back to The

19

Ship, only a stone's throw away, for his customary pint.

As we crossed the level-crossing approaching the Inn a solution to my problem suddenly presented itself. I suggested to my companion that when we reached The Ship he would pop in and buy a couple of large bottles of his favourite beer, whilst I took care of 'Enery and we could then have it in comfort by his own fireside. "I'll pay for them," I added, "and then you can tell me a bit more about that son-in-law of yours – on your own admission I might have been one of the family anyway, so I ought to know." It seemed that my last few words, and the free beverage promised, finally decided him. And so, I slowly walked 'Enery home and we had barely reached his little cottage before Reuben caught us up, and in no time we were seated round a small but brightly glowing fire.

'Enery was soon fast asleep in his chair and Reuben, having procured three pint beer glasses, proceeded to fill two of these, nodding towards the sleeping figure, "'is can wait."

"Not for me," I said. "I'm off home as soon as you tell me about your son-in-law and I'm teetotal anyhow." Reuben laughed.

"Aye there's some as likes a drop an' some as don't, which is only as it should be, and leaves more for 'em what does, if yer gits me meanin'." And with a chuckle he finished both glasses.

A few minutes passed by, but I knew it was useless to hurry him. Eventually I said, "What about your son-in-law, how did you manage it?"

Reuben's eyes twinkled at the memory. "Well it took a tidy while to git shot o' 'im. He was that obstinit, so I say's to meself, I'll make things that uncomfortable for him as 'e'll want to git out. So, one mornin a-fore 'e's up I saws a little bit off the bottom of one of his chair legs, not much, just a little bit, to make it rock about so as he couldn't sit comftible like. But when I gits back, there 'e was as comftible as yer like with a big 'eaded nail drove up into it, to make up for what I'd cut off. It was a'scraping and a'chewing into me floorboards and I wished then I 'adn't dun it. Likewise, the more I see'd o' 'im the more I couldn't abide 'im sittin' there. So, when me coal run out, I didn't buy no more, nor chop no wood, and next day when he does git up, 'e sez, 'Where's the fire?' And I sez, 'There ain't going to be no fire, no more. I'm a'going up to me bedroom an' if I wants a fire, that's where it'll be.'

"But next day when I gits 'ome from The Ship there 'e is sitting right across the front o' a nicely burning grate which he'd got me daughter, Annie, to git, cos he told her that I'd run out o' coal, and she'd bought a sack. It weren't till after I found it were charged to me. So, when I gits me chair to sit as near as 'e would let me git, he says, 'You can git away from my fire, yours is upstairs like you said.' Well it made me so roaring mad as I packed up there and then, slammed the door so 'ard as to bring a bit of ceiling down, and went up to me bedroom to think a bit more what to do.

"But no-wise could I think 'ow to git rid o' 'im, an' I weren't strong enough now like I was once to chuck 'im out neck and crop. 'Sides, I didn't want to upset me daughter too much, being as she was a'wedded to 'im. So it looked as though I was stuck with 'im for good. And me pushed out of me own front room, afore me time as well. An' that was 'ow it was and likely to be so as far as I could see.

"But it weren't to a week or two after, when me daughter, Annie, comes home from her 'char-in' at the 'all and tells me that Charley, me old mate's 'widder' had passed away that I got to thinking agin. I keeps me own council and later on when I gits back from paying me last respects and seeing what sort of fun-ral they give 'er, Annie wants to know all about it. I tells 'er that being it was a Parish burial an' no kith nor kin, nor flowers, to bid her good-bye, it weren't hardly worth the walk up the 'ill and 'er with all that money stowed away, secret like, what she never knewed about.

"I thought that lazy ****** of a son-in-law was asleep but he soon waked up when I spoke o' money.

'What money?' sez he.

'Never you mind,' sez I. 'I've said too much already, cos I thought you was asleep and not concerned in me private conversation wiv me own daughter.' So, he sits an' sulks until it's 'is time to go out, which he does by slamming the front door, loud, an' then I hears the floorboards a'creaking as 'e come back, to listen. Me daughter comes back to the talk we was havin' and sez, 'What money?'

"I knowed as how he were all ears just outside, so I sez, 'I ain't so sure I should be a 'telling on it but if yer don' t breave not one word to no one and least of all to that good for nothing lazy b***** of a husband of yawn,' which I sed nice and loud, 'then I'll tell 'ee.'

"So, I moved over a bit closer to the door, an' I tells her how, one day, just before he died, Charley comes to me, opens his tool bag, and out pours a lot of coins, all stamped with the 'ead of a Queen, and to my knowledge we ain't had a Queen for a tidy few years, so they must be old, and they was all shiny like as if they was gold. An' he tells me as how 'e'd bin doing a bit of carpentering in an old cottage along Leigh High Street and comes across 'em stowed away behind some bricks, what was covered by a bit o' panerlin'. The cottage being sort o' empty, 'e helps hisself to 'em an' don't see why he should tell the landlord, nor yet his gov'ner, cos as he sez, 'Findings, Keepings.' But 'e don't know what he ought to do wiv 'em so he comes to see me, for me to tell 'im, us being sich old mates tergether. An' I tells 'im, 'Take 'em 'ome and 'ide 'em nice and safe until a bit later, cos if the landlord of the cottage or maybe them customs people got to 'ear, they'd be ar-ter 'im faster than chasing a winkle up a clamshell gut, and on no account tell 'is missus, else it 'ould be all over Leigh in no time a'tall.'

"He died soon ar-ter an' I've bin thinkin' for a long time about 'em. Maybe wur've a tidy bit now, an' I tells Annie it's all betwix 'er an' me, an' not to drop a word to no one, least o' all to that no good husband o' 'ers, – hoping as 'e was still a'listenin'."

"'Enery stirred from his slumber and sounds issued through his beard. "He sez he wants 'is dinner," confided Reuben.

I could plainly see that my chance of Reuben finishing his story was slipping away, so I suggested, "Why not give him a glass of beer to tide him over. I don't want to go home without hearing the last bit."

"Aye, I'll try that," said Reuben. He bent over as 'Enery cupped his ear and shouted, "What about a glass o' beer fust." Nods and jerks indicated that 'Enery was agreeable. So, with a threequarters filled glass, because as Reuben explained, "'is 'and shakes all the top outer it an' gits wasted", 'Enery was soon dozing off again with that peculiar tranquillity that sometimes comes with age. Reuben once more resumed his story.

"Well next morning ar-ter I tells Annie, I finds me son-in-law up an' dressed in his Sunday best, an' instead of a'blockin' up the fireplace he goes out without so much as a word as to where he might be a-goin'. An' when he gits back ar-ter dinner, 'e's all smirks and grins an' looks that cunnin' as yer wouldn't believe. An' when I sez to Annie at teatime I was a-thinkin' o' goin' along to see Charley's widder's lan'lord wiv a view to me movin' in, and me an 'Enery livin' in it to git a bit of peace and quiet, up he jumps an' sez:

'Yer too late, you old ******.' 'Yus,' 'e sez, 'Yer too late. I was-n't a-goin' to tell yer but yer might as well know 'ere and now as I've bin to see the lan'lord, an' arranged to move in next week. An' what's more I've got the key an' yer won't be welcome to set foot in it, cos I've had enough o' yer bossie ways a-runnin' me life.' And then he sez, all clever-like, 'B'sides, I knows what I knows, and there's some as I won't mention don't think I knows what I knows, and I ain't a'tellin', so stuff that in yer pipe.'

"Well, sure enough, next week 'e moves out, which was not soon enough for me, an' I jist couldn't believe 'e'd gorn, and 'Enery 'ere," he indicated the still sleeping figure, "moved in a'long o' me, an' yer can see for yerself, he ain't no trouble, 'sept for a bit o' waiting on when Annie ain't around. An' 'e's got a tidy bit put away wiv no one to have it when 'e's gone, 'sept Annie an' me for takin' care on 'im.

"It were jist like Heaven ar-ter I see'd the last of 'im, until Annie comes in a couple o' days later a-crying her eyes out, an' lets on how he'd pulled up nigh on all the floorboards an' was starting to pull down the fireplace and chimney, and the next time I see's 'er, he'd fallen through the ceiling in the bedroom, which was all down on 'er bed, cos of his climbing about in the roof.

"She sez as 'ow she couldn't live there no longer an' was a-livin'-in up at the 'all. She knowed now, what 'e was ar-ter and couldn't find, an' swore on 'er oath as she niver breathed a word to him, but I keeps me own council. 'Least said soonest mended,' as me old mum used to say.

"The Lord above knows what'll 'appen when 'is landlord calls for 'is rent and see's what e's bin up to; put 'im in prison most like-ly. An' a judgement on 'im for his goings on 'ere and trying to pinch a poor widder's money, which was rightly 'ers."

As though speaking his thoughts aloud, Reuben added, "An' what she didn't know about, nei-ver."

I didn't quite follow this line of reasoning but let it pass.

'Enery was showing signs of life again and his shrill, treble tone, accompanied by agitated nods and jerks again interrupted the continuation of Reuben's story.

"'E sez he wants 'is dinner. I best git 'im some afore Annie gits 'ere, an' a bit for meself as well. I've telled yer best part of 'ow he was got ridden of, enough as is good for yer to know, but I'll allus be pleased to see yer anytime, now yer knows where I lives and there's room for yer to sit near the fire." He added the last bit with relish. "So I'll be seein' yer out. But jist 'old on a minute whilst I go upstairs to me bedroom."

The minute multiplied itself to several minutes. 'Enery's plaintive voice was again in evidence calling for his dinner when Reuben, having carefully descended the tiny spiral staircase, walked the half dozen steps along the tiny passage and opened the street door ready for my departure. On the step he pressed a small round coin into my hand. "'Ere's a little keepsake for yer. Got lots more upstairs. I knows as 'ow you'll keep yer mouth shut. Being like you was nearly a relative o' mine, and wouldn't git an old man into trouble. An' after all, 'Findings, Keepings.' Ain't they?"

As I said goodbye, I heard him say, "Too late, 'e tells me, maybe I was the day afore, for me tea, but I knowed where Charley hid 'em."

I shut the small front gate. "Give me kind regards to yer Aunt Polly," he called. "See yer termorrer."

3

A Helping Hand

The days of winter melted into weeks and they in turn to months, but with that complete disregard to the value of time that we completely ignore in our youth, I neglected to answer the quiet but still persistent urge to renew my acquaintance with Reuben again.

My footsteps, by force of habit, led me always eastwards, towards Chalkwell. I rarely now visited the old town and then only to get my immediate needs of boat gear and fittings.

I thought of him often, as I did my Auntie Polly. It had become somehow connected, both with her and my Dad, and I had begun to accept him almost as family, as he claimed he might have been.

But also, like Auntie, and my other elderly relatives, I sadly neglected them, and my own immediate needs and interests filled my life (something I now look back on with sorrow and a deep regret), and consequently it was almost early spring before I had made the effort to call on him.

A week or so previously, Auntie wanted a bit of carpentry done for her, something that I never minded, as while just talking to pass the time seemed so non-productive, never realising its value to the old and lonely, I was always willing to help her in a practical way.

I told her of my meeting with Reuben, and her eyes awakened with memories. "So he wished to be remembered, did he. Well I haven't forgotten him, tell him. I knew he had his eye on me, but he had a bad influence on your Dad. Not that your Dad needed much help in that direction, and I wasn't going to encourage him or let him get his hands on me, like some of the other girls he knew. But, for all that, he was a handsome young fellow and maybe I *was* a bit short with him. But things were different in those days. Give him my best regards and tell him I haven't forgotten, and should he care to walk up the hill, there's a cup of tea waiting for him."

I knew this would please him, and possibly salve my conscience with an excuse for my shameful neglect, and with this added incentive, a few days later my footsteps once more led me to the door of his cottage, accompanied by a bag containing a bottle of "tonic", as a thanks offering.

I was shocked, how in such a short while age had ravished him. He walked with difficulty, aided by a stick. A stick that I felt I had seen before, its dog head worn but still carved in exquisite beauty. His eyes, still bright and full of mischief, still remained in the frail body, and he welcomed me with obvious delight and no sign of reproach at my long absence. Inside, the little room seemed even brighter and better kept than previously, although even then never untidy. I gave him Auntie's message, but saw no hope of its fulfilment. He would never walk Leigh Hill again, but the thought pleased him. He pointed to a vacant chair, 'Enery's chair, but now empty. 'Enery no longer had use for it, he had "passed on", Reuben informed me with a genuine affection in his voice, a few weeks after I last visited, but he didn't seem to recognise how long that was, and I was thankful for it.

Once seated, he inquired how life in general was treating me. I did my best to satisfy him, but our lives were too far apart to meet on level ground. Besides, it was his knowledge of Dad and those early days in Old Leigh that were my interest.

I got no further than on the previous occasions, but then in some mysterious way, our conversation came back to "that son-in-law of mine", and immediately my old curiosity was aroused.

Unlike previously, I sensed he was a little loath to discuss him, but once started, he was the Reuben I knew.

"It'll take a long time a telling, an' as yer know, I get that thirsty as yer wouldn't believe, a telling on it." He eyed the bottle I had brought. "If it's all the same to you, I'll have a glass, jist to wet me whistle so to speak," and promptly put words into action. This duly accomplished, he then produced a fine gold watch, consulted it, then proceeded with his "a tellin' of it".

"Well, as yer can well imagine, it weren't that long afore tongues got a-waggin'. All that noise of banging and knocking fair got up the snouts of 'is neighbours, and when Annie left him to live-in up at-the 'all, there was a tidy to-do an' noses poking in all over, an' I'm telling folk that 'e was a repairing an' doing up the property which no one believed cos he was that bone lazy as they all knowed. 'E wouldn't lift a finger to do nothin', not for 'isself, let alone for 'is landlord, who wasn't that long in a finding out some-thin' was a-goin' on there. And when we sees what he'd done, he was that mad, he goes straight up to the police station, and takes out a summons agin him for wilful damage to his property, and the case come up at Chelmsford Court a few weeks later. I went over wiv Annie and one or two more Leigh men to see how he got on, and poor Annie nigh broke down at the sight of him in the dock, and the Magistrate sez to him, and why, my man, did yer do this wilful damage to yer landlord's property, and he sez as h'ed lost somefing and was a looking for it and couldn't find it. The Magistrate said, if every tenant pulled his landlord's property to bits every time he'd lost somefing, no landlord could sleep peaceful o'nights, and no tenant a house fit to live in, and fined him fifty pun or three months "hard" if he couldn't pay, which of course he couldn't. An' that's where he is now, and lord knows what he'd do when he gits out, as he ain't coming here agin, not if I knows it."

He paused, filled his glass, "Ain't no good askin yer to have one, I knows so I'll help meself agin if yer don't mind. Ain't no good Annie expecting me to have him here, she's a looking after me now, since 'Enery was called, an lays at rest in Leigh Cemetry, specially as she's given up her char-in and I keeps her."

He looked around his little room, "Aye, and a tidy job she does, everything kept bright an' shiny and in its place. I have to wipe me boots every time I comes in now, but she's a good gal, and thanks to 'Enery I'll be able to look after her when I'm gone. Cos like I sez, his as had no one in the world to leave it to, except me or Annie, does jist that. He makes his will and leaves all he's got to me for life and Annie after I'm gone, which was a little bit of property and the bits and pieces he had here, like his gold watch an' walking stick, which has come in right handy jist now, and his clothes which I gives away as they'd no ways fit me, and a leather bag wiv some sovrins, I ain't a tellin how many, in his drawer upstairs. It was them what was the answer to me worries what had been worrying me, ever since I got that lot of coins from where Charley hid them, cos arter I got them I didn't know, no more than Charley did, what to do wiv them, or how much they was werf. So I hides them, like I told Charlie to do, and then get to worrying about them."

"I think maybe that son-in-law of mine, when he can't find them in his place, would've cottened on as I've got them in here, so I stops in all day a minding of them an' never gits out to The Ship nor nowheres, and Annie keeps saying, ain't yer going out, you're in me way all the time when I'm a tidying. So I gets a bag and puts them in, wiv an empty beer bottle on top, and goes out, an all the time I'm afraid of losing it, or putting it down and people gets to talking as to what might be in it. If I leaves it at home, I'm afeared as Annie might find it, as while I told her about them I hadn't told her as how I had them. So I takes them back again and hides them as I had in the first place under the floorboards of my bedroom, and still worries what to do with them.

"Then I comes to thinking, maybe as that son-in-law might open his mouth too much to one of them a-thieving mates of his in Chelmsford jailhouse. The Lord above knows what he might get up to, and me a frighted to say a word to anyone for fear of them finding out, and wished maybe as you'd come to see me, as you being the only one what hadn't got an axe to grind and could keep his mouth shut. I'd ask you what you thinks to do wiv them, and us being kind of nearly related and all. Then along comes old 'Enery and lends me a helping hand."

I interrupted, "I thought you said Henry had died?"

"Aye, so I did and so he was, but it didn't stop him a helping me cos when I found them sovrins I knew as I could use them and spend them and no questions asked, what was more than I could wiv them other coins." So I changes them over, and fills up the bag wiv them instead. When later the lawyer man comes along to explain 'Enery's will, like he wrote to say he was, I had them a ready alongside 'Enery's other effects, like his gold watch and stick an sich like, and tells him as I found them in 'Enery's drawer upstairs. And very interested he were too, and he sez it's very strange as 'Enery 'ad never told him about them, and I sez, nor me neiver, what wasn't so queer after all, seeing as he'd never knowed about them in the first place.

"Then he says, in my opinion, they were worth a lot of money, and wiv your permission, as of course under the terms of Mr. 'Enery White's will, they are now your property. I will take them up to "Lunnon" and get them valued and if you so wish sell them by auction in the City. Of course, I'll give you a recipy for them."

"A receipt", I interrupted.

"That's what I said, a recipy for them, which he did wiv a stamp and his signature. All above board so to speak, and now I'm a waiting to hear from him, and what's more got rid of them thanks to a helping hand from me old mate 'Enery, cos if he'd knowed, and maybe he do, it were him as done it, for me."

He paused and poked the fire into life.

"Well, I suppose you best be a getting along, Annie'll be here any minute, and start a stirrin' things up. I'll jist pop upstairs afore I sees you out. Got a little something for you."

I waited, expecting perhaps another coin as a keepsake, but this time, wrapped in a piece of sailcloth, while still round, it was much larger.

"It's me silver watch. I've got 'Enery's gold one now, and I'd sooner you had it as anyone, seeing as you was nearly me nephew, an' I thinks of you as family. Give me kind regards to your Auntie Polly."

He led me to the door and ushered me out. As I reached the front gate, I heard him call, "See yer termorrer".

I didn't see him 'termorrer', or for that matter any further 'termorrers'. Shortly after our last meeting, he joined 'Enery in Leigh Cemetery, and I have little doubt that when he reaches the Golden Gates, his list of sins will be long. But I am sure St. Peter will look the other way as he slips in, and I have an uneasy feeling that as he passes through he'll look back and down on me and call "See yer termorrer".

4

At the End of the Rainbow

Strangely enough, although quite unknown to me at the time, in another part of Leigh a search involving wealth that went far beyond the wildest dreams of either my old friend Reuben and his long-suffering daughter Annie's "no good" husband was being pursued with equal vigour and dedication, but with much less noise and destruction and certainly not the unfortunate ending that accompanied the efforts of his son-in-law.

But let me start at the beginning, which has no bearing at all on my story, other than to acquaint the reader with a general background and to those interested in Old Leigh.

When the railway came to Leigh around 1854-56, it destroyed, divided and effectively cut much of the Old Town of Leigh, that rested on the small amount of flat land that existed at the bottom, from the grass and cultivated slopes that led up to the equally flat fields of what is now the Leigh of today.

The only remaining lane, or road, in Old Leigh, other than Horse Hill, the High Street and Billet Lane, was a hedge and ditch-lined track running closely parallel with the new railroad on the north side, known as Hogs Lane owing, as legend has it, to the number of pigs that were kept there.

This lane, with the coming of the railway and the general development that naturally accrued later, became New Road, and development spread up the slopes, and joined the ever increasing building boom in the New Leigh above.

Many rows of small terrace houses built by property speculators was the result, and in spite of their age, many are still standing, and with modernisation, still good comfortable homes. But there was a period when age and the depression of the early thirties allowed many to fall into disrepair and the streets became poor and neglected.

It was in such a street – with rusting railings, broken or non-existing gates and peeling paintwork – of gentile poverty that I found myself in the cold misty dampness of late November.

The twilight was closing in, as by the feeble yellow glow of one of the few undamaged street lamps I finally tracked the house I was looking for. I knew the younger brother of the person living there, and in a moment of generosity, I had offered to help out and do a small repair job for him, but as matters turned out, it never materialised.

The steps from the pavement took me to a narrow alcove, it would have been an exaggeration to call it a porch. The door, after a little searching, revealed a knocker, on which I quietly knocked, without acknowledgement, but a louder one had better results, as a distant voice, somewhere inside, said "come in", and to my surprise, the door yielded to my pressure. Obviously no fear of thieves or burglars haunted the inhabitants hereabouts. I found myself in an extension of the long passage in front of me, at the end of which, a thin ribbon of light outlined a door topped by a fanlight similarly illuminated.

I waited, some little time elapsed, and then a voice called, "I said come in."

Walking carefully, or perhaps feeling my way would be more accurate, I reached the ribbon of light, knocked and pushed open the door. The scene still lives in my memory. The overall impression was of a general greyness; it seemed the outside mist and grey of the street had invaded and settled permanently inside also. The grey of the moth-eaten curtains, daring anyone to touch through age, the mantelpiece overloaded with its contents, the fireplace and general woodwork of a similar grey, was an indication that the chimney had not seen a sweep for many a long year. It was plain that no woman's hand had ever been permitted to attack the layer of dust that covered most of the contents of the room, warmed more by the lacework pattern of pale light around the top of an ancient paraffin stove, than the heat it was supposed to give.

Under the light of a naked, dirty electric light bulb that hung from the ceiling, sat a little grey man at a large table. His face, grey from lack of health and sunlight, thin grey hair brushed across his balding head, but with a fringe of lank straggly hair overhanging the collar of a greyish jacket, all blended together in the pale light.

This reflected on his steel rimmed glasses, completing the half I could see of him, and revealed the utter chaos of his surroundings.

The table was piled at one end with large tattered leather bound books, still revealing traces of green binding and worn gold lettering. An ancient document, held down by an equally ancient magnifying glass, lay in front of him. Inks, pens, rubbers and other oddments on a tray, bits of paper, containing names, graphs and much I couldn't see, exercise books in abundance, are things I remember. But more perhaps the floor. Large sheets of what I thought was white ceiling lining paper, carpeted odd sections of the floor, mostly covered with lines and names of what I now know to be family pedigrees and all the paraphernalia involved in family history backed up by a miscellaneous assortment of family photographs, smaller books and heraldic signs in little frames on shelves in the chimney breast alcoves. To this day I can recall it all, imprinted like a photograph in my memory in almost exact detail.

I started to explain my business, but it was dismissed almost immediately, as if of no consequence, and probably seeing the look of curiosity and surprise I could hardly hide, he launched into a torrent of words with all the pent up volume of those that have not spoken to a fellow human for days. Quite obviously his mind had neither room nor time except for this one all-powerful interest or perhaps more correctly, obsession, he was involved in.

It needed little encouragement on my part, a willing listener was all he wanted. Just how willing on my side, I had no time to consider.

It seemed, from what I remember, that it was all the fault of William the Conqueror, or at least he started it, by allowing my host's descendants to accompany him on his little trip to England and decided for the benefit of its inhabitants to stay for good. If he, out of the goodness of his heart, hadn't given most, if not all the inhabitants' ground and land to his friends, all would have been well.

Having once acquired this kindly gift of someone else's land, all that remained was to look after it, and this, my informant's ancestors did, losing occasional bits and pieces as time went on. The only problem was that by the time it reached his grandfather, what was left, no one quite knew who or what belonged to anybody. But he still possessed a sizeable manor house and large estate in Essex a few miles from London. From then on it was a story of long leases, no wills or none found, litigation, chancery and much else I couldn't follow, and eventually bankruptcy that led to an early grave for his father. All this was carefully explained and detailed for me, from one of the huge sheets of diagrams and names rescued from its resting place on the floor until I eventually lost track. But out of politeness I kept nodding wisely at right and frequent intervals.

Taking over as eldest son, and equally assured that he was entitled to the estate, occupied, he claimed unlawfully, by tenants on a hundred year lease, and now holding title under some obscure law, he carried on with his father's claim. This meant more searching, more litigation, but step by step nearer to proving his rights to this astronomically increasing land value estate, now almost on the outskirts of London's spread.

I gathered that the discovery of the two documents, or perhaps either, would substantiate and prove his claim, and a fortune was within sight.

Eventually, in a mental whirl at the monumental effort involved, with so much I couldn't follow, I left him, I think, a little happier, that he had found someone to talk to and listen. I went again down that long dark passage into the outside world of damp November mist. My own mission completely ignored, I could only think how chance or fate, call it what you will, makes playthings of us all. Here was a man, living in abject poverty, lonely, cold and most likely hungry, with almost less than the necessities of life, who, if his claim was justified, and I had little doubt it was, should be living a life of luxury in a manor house, surrounded by a fortune in land of many acres. But somehow I had the feeling it didn't really matter to him all that much now, if he could only prove himself right and his claim justified.

I never saw him again.

At a bus stop, just recently, I met his youngest brother. He had grown a little grey man, almost a copy of the elder one. I asked after his brother, only to be told, as I almost expected, that he had passed on some few years back. Had he been successful in his quest, I enquired, realising almost immediately that it was a foolish question. It was plain he hadn't benefited by his brother's demise. But in answer to my question, he explained he had taken over from

33

where his elder brother had left off, and was continuing the search. His wife had left him, he was now on his own and living in his brother's house. No, he hadn't found the all-important missing documents, but hopefully suggested he had some further leads that could just possibly help. Tapping the briefcase under his arm, he said he was just returning from the records office in London where his brother had spent, he told me, most of his life.

I said it might take a long time, even now, but to cheer him up, added that the value of the land must be increasing beyond all reason – certainly hundreds of thousands at least, when it eventually became his. For a moment his face lit up, as if his dream had really become fact.

My bus was coming, I said quickly, and what if you never find those documents? He looked a bit uncertain, "Well . . ." he paused for a moment then said, "I have a nephew, he's a bright lad and seems interested. I've shown him what I'm doing and got him started, and he helps me quite a bit, and . . ."

I didn't catch the last few words as I scrambled for my bus. "Cheerio and good luck," I called back, as the bus left, much as I left his brother those many years back, and once again I wondered at the fate that plays with our lives. No wonder the gods look down and laugh as they shuffle their human playthings across the chess board of life.

Two, or maybe only one, pieces of paper, between poverty and riches, and most likely yet another human toy to play with, to replace those counted out. The trap was already baited, with land prices still rocketing. A crock of gold, only just two documents away and the end of the rainbow within sight. Well maybe . . .

POSTSCRIPT

A neighbour has just told me how a friend of his bought for a few shillings at a local auction an old picture that took his fancy. When he got home, he decided to replace the dirty brown paper backing and found between the picture and the backing a will. While it had no connection with the above story, it shows that anything can happen and truth is stranger than fiction. Incidentally it cleared up a long-standing dispute, altered quite a lot of lives and the finder received a very substantial gift from those who benefited.

5

Pandora's Box

I have an uneasy feeling that this story has crept into the book without invitation. It is short, has no central figure or character, vague in facts and an unsatisfactory ending of its accuracy.

I can only assume my reason for writing it lies in my previous experience, when I contemplated the strange ways fate or chance plays in our lives. And to the even stranger fact that occasionally, when it does decide to become generous and reward someone – for as far as I can see, doing nothing to deserve it – becomes so unexpected that it passes by unrecognised.

And one such case comes to mind.

I had long before left the Beach, the Second World War was over and I was now in partnership with my younger brother in the building trade, not of large estates, just here and there, mostly on the small plots of land that still remained in the town. And for this reason we found ourselves building a small house in Lymington Avenue, Leigh.

We were made very welcome by our immediate neighbours, among them a well known and respected member of an Old Leigh fishing family, then retired. He became a frequent visitor, his hobby was my hobby also, breeding canaries and other birds, and I in turn visited him and his aviary, and this is his story.

They had been trawling past the Maplin Sands at low waters and he saw a yellow object on the edge of the tide, and ever watchful for a bit of salvage, his mate jumped into the dinghy, went ashore and secured it. It was a strong metal box, firmly and strongly locked. At the time, they were unable to open it, which increased their curiosity even more, and added to their frustration. So when they reached the Ray, they moored and duly cooked their catch of shrimps, then turned once again with coal hammer and chisel to attack and open their find.

With more and more impatience they struggled to get it open, and at last the mangled lid gave way, only to find, to their extreme disappointment, all it contained was a canvas bag, filled with what looked like grit or small shingle. They emptied it on the deck, and there it lay, their hopes of a valuable find and all their efforts shattered. It got walked on, spread around, kicked about, and finally, sluiced overboard with the final washing down of decks before leaving.

That would have been the end of the story, except, as he told me – discussing the mystery of the strange box he had found, with a more knowledgable man – he was informed that the contents of the canvas bag were, in all probability, "Industrial Diamonds". So somewhere in the sands of the Ray, or maybe on the foreshore, little bits of a fortune still exist.

And the story didn't end there either. It has been suggested that it is connected with the death in mysterious circumstance of that well known and popular lady aviator of pre-War fame, then Miss Amy Johnson, and later Mrs. Amy Morrison. Her strange death in a terrible storm over the Thames Estuary has never been satisfactorily explained. As a member of an elite corps of trained pilots not operating in actual combat, but actively engaged in auxiliary duties – such as ferrying and transporting personnel etc. – it was an invaluable addition to our Air Force.

Witnesses claim to have seen her aircraft in great difficulty and distress, momentarily through the blinding rain and sleet, as it forced its way through the storm. They also claim to have seen *two* bodies or objects leave the plane, although it was claimed by the Air Ministry and those whose business it was to know, that she was supposed to have been alone and they had no knowledge of a second passenger.

Suffice to say, the machine never reached its destination and was never found or heard of again, or its pilot (or passenger?), and no doubt, with the secrecy that surrounded all wartime operations, the whole event is shrouded in mystery and rumour. Among these rumours, it was suggested that the object of her journey was to deliver a cargo, among other things of "Industrial Diamonds", to a secret and unidentified rendezvue in a foreign country.

I make no claims as to its accuracy, I am repeating only odd bits of rumour and hearsay, which, added together, seems to make sense. Or was it just coincidence?

6

Saving "Sinners"

When my self-appointed "Uncle" Reuben, and to a lesser degree 'Enery, departed this life, my few links with Old Leigh, other than business, were finally severed.

Those of my father's generation were practically all gone, and those Old Towners of my schooldays were not close, and outnumbered by the increasing numbers of the children of the residents at the top of the hill. An undefinable line of class distinction, while not in particular evidence, was still there, or maybe perhaps we just chose our friends from those living in our vicinity. So although my roots were in the Old Town and I grew up with them, my sympathies and interests were with the newcomers and unlike my father, was not one of them, and as I grew older, my footsteps led me in the opposite direction, Chalkwell. I lost complete touch, and in any case, had little reason to believe there was still part, or at least a connection to Reuben's story, that still remained unknown to me.

It was many years after. I was walking along Leigh Broadway when I chanced to meet a girl friend of my youth accompanied by a more elderly lady. I was pleased to see her, it was so long since we last met. I made the usual niceties of conversation, and then she turned to her companion, introducing her. "You remember Annie". Memory flooded back, "of course," I replied, although if truth was known, I hadn't recognised her company as the Annie I knew, but I was pleased to see her and I think it was mutual. We spoke for a few minutes on old times, and then quite naturally, I asked news of her husband, and for the first time, realised I never knew his name. The constant irritation of Reuben's old age, he always referred to him as "that there son-in-law of mine", and I remember how once when I asked, he had said, "I never calls him by his name, it would choke me," and having no wish to provoke such a catastrophe, I left it at that. I felt, immediately I asked, that I was "treading on forbidden ground". Her answer was short and to the point.

"Oh Him. He's gone." And it was plain that further reference to the subject was unwelcome. I took the hint, with a vague feeling that all was not as it should be.

Our conversation then returned to the usual memories of old times, the amazing changes of the town etc. We reached Leigh Church, where Annie, after having said her goodbyes, parted from us down Church Hill and home. I turned to my companion, "So Annie's a widow now."

"Well she is and she isn't, she doesn't rightly know," was her reply.

"That's a bit of a contradiction, she must be one or the other, surely," I said.

"So you might well think," was my companion's answer. "Look, I live just along Rectory Grove, come and have a cup of tea with me, and I'll tell you all about it. I'm surprised you haven't heard. Almost all of Old Leigh knows, and a tidy lot up here as well. There was a bit in the paper too, but it was kept pretty quiet, for all that, and it finished the Brethren."

Even if I had wanted to (and I didn't) I could see there was going to be an interesting story, and shortly afterwards, was seated in a comfortable chair, with a cup of tea to hand and my friend opposite. This is a summary of her tale.

His sentence served, Annie's husband returned to Leigh a thinner and wiser man. Certainly a lot "more wiser" said some. He was received with mixed feelings, not knowing the reasons for the damage he had done, but an intense dislike for landlords in general excused much of it, with some, and in others a curiosity at his foolishness in destroying what seemed a comfortable little home puzzled them. All agreed his sentence was harsh, but no one liked him enough to help him in a practical manner. Each drew their own conclusions and left it at that.

Reuben had not the slightest intention of allowing him to occupy his now peaceful home and fireside, and he said so in no uncertain terms, and left no doubts that was the way he was going to keep it.

Annie was torn both ways, her father or her husband. Her position was perhaps the worst of all, but she solved it by going up to "The Hall" where she was well liked and succeeded in getting the Master to give her husband a job and a corner in the "great barn" to live until he could find suitable accommodation elsewhere. So for the moment, the situation was solved and all was well.

Meanwhile, a couple of years previous to all this domestic upset in Reuben's home life, events, totally unconnected – but already destined to make Annie and her husband part of the ingredients with them, in the unpredictable mixing bowl of the future – were taking place in one of the small villas a few hundred yards from where I was now seated with my friend.

A breakaway group, from a Non-Conformist Church, just outside the Parish calling themselves the Brethren of the Reformation, led by a fanatical evangelist (but he certainly had no recognisable connection with Martin Luther) had established themselves in Leigh at the villa mentioned, and it wasn't long before their neighbours were aware of their presence. Sundays and Wednesday evenings became unbearable, as with voice, organ and religious enthusiasm they tore apart the peace of the quiet street, praising their Maker with loud and joyous abandon. No plot of vacant land was too small for them to take their banners and address any of the locals prepared to listen. Many were the loud "Hosannas", "Hallelujahs", and "Praise The Lord", acknowledging those, who at various intervals, broke into the message of their leader to express their overwhelming faith and undying belief in their cause.

When later, a "rag-time" band, with hymns suitable adjusted to that latest style of modern music, was included in their gatherings, the sect grew and flourished in a quite remarkable manner, especially amongst the young. Much to the relief of those in the vicinity of their meeting house – which was now quite incapable of holding such a large congregation – they moved to the very barn that was Annie's husband's temporary residence. It was loaned by the kind-hearted farmer for their Sunday and midweek gatherings, and mostly with only cows or horses to suffer the brunt of their efforts. Antagonism died down and they were received into the community, if not with enthusiasm, at least with tolerance.

It was here the mixing-bowl began to stir its contents. A "sinner" in the shape of the barn's single occupant was crying out to be "saved", or so it seemed, and there was nothing the leader of the Brethren loved more than saving a "sheep that had strayed from the fold". On hearing his story, the leader immediately set about saving his soul from the Devil and damnation, even to the extent of giving him the small back bedroom in the aforesaid villa, to be near at hand to ward off any temptations that might assail him in the course of his salvation.

His efforts were not wasted. In fact it amazed everybody who knew Annie's spouse, how remarkably he responded to being "saved", how much a comfortable bed, good food, and the congregation's prayers and goodwill – which included a new suit and a little financial help – had to do with his reformation. Nobody doubted it, the change was there to see, and quite soon he was an example to all, a constant joy to his Benefactor and proof, if proof was needed, of the power of prayer. It warmed and comforted the hearts of those around him that their efforts would not go unnoticed when their turn came to render an account on the Day of Judgement.

It seemed no one was more grateful for being "shown the light" than "The Sinner" himself. He sang louder, put in more Hallelujahs and Hosannas than any other at all the meetings and gatherings. At every available opportunity, he would spring up and inform the congregation how he, a miserable sinner, had been saved from eternal darkness and how they also could be saved, should they so wish.

Both he and the Brethren prospered. On Reuben's demise he returned to the cottage and occupied, not 'Enery's chair, but that of Reuben's. To show his unselfishness, and that Annie had no particular right to it, he gave her 'Enery's, and allowed her to wait on him in the manner he considered his due as Master of the House. The fire burned as cheerfully for him as it had previously for Reuben.

The cottage, now Annie's, and the little legacy she had inherited, made it unnecessary for him to work. After all, how could he? His time, now fully occupied with the affairs of the Brethren, was more important. Dressed now in a quiet semi-clerical suit, no one was more assiduous in visiting the old and sick, distributing leaflets, helping good causes, and even on occasions, giving his leader a break and taking his place with a newly found eloquence, almost out-doing his sponsor in promises of the joy to come.

The barn, cold and draughty, was no place for the now respectable and increasing gatherings of the sect. A more luxurious, warm and comfortable chapel was contemplated. Land was secured by a small deposit, plans drawn and submitted, estimates requested and all responsibilities cheerfully accepted by him. In fact he assumed complete control over the whole project, Secretary, Treasurer and Planner. Helped with a substantial legacy from one of the members who conveniently "passed on", the building fund took shape, beyond the wildest dreams of those who had sponsored it, and eventually reached around £9,000, a fortune in those days, and all was set to start.

It was about this time when the now-important Secretary had need to pack his bags for a conference of Non-Conformist Ministers and Chapel-goers to meet in their annual get-together on the south coast, and Annie and one or two of the members saw him off from Leigh Station.

Nobody worried when the week passed with no word, no doubt his time was fully occupied. He was never seen again, or the building fund. It was surprising what a lot he *had* learned in Chelmsford.

I have hesitated at continuing this story lest I be accused of unnecessary preoccupation with Annie's erring husband. But I feel it should be told. His disappearance was a "Seven Day Wonder" in Leigh but quietly "Hushed Up". It was soon forgotten, as was the complete break up of the chapel.

The Elders each laid blame at his "Brother's" door for the catastrophe that had descended on them. The scandalised congregation, with the loss of their fund, fell apart. Their leader, disillusioned and heartbroken by his protege, left for pastures a-new. And so it ended.

The whole story, now in the dim and distant past, was forgotten and, as I said previously, he was never seen or heard of again. Or was he?

And that is why I have reservations in resurrecting this story any further. It is of no benefit to anyone. My only excuse is that it would make it more complete, and it all started when I received the following letter a few months ago, dated 2nd April 1980.

Dear Arthur,

I trust you are well. You will be surprised to hear from me but I would be glad if you can call, at the above address when convenient, as I have found something that might interest you.

Best Wishes
Yours Sincerely
Hilda

Who was Hilda? Intrigued and puzzled I couldn't wait. I didn't know anyone at that address or road as far as I knew. So that very afternoon I made my way to the writer's home, only to be greeted by my old friend that I had last met with Annie, those years before. She had moved, her old home was now demolished, and the site occupied by a large modern post office. But she still kept in touch with Annie.

From her new residence, a short distance away, ashamed at my lack of memory, we soon found comfort of a cup of tea. I asked after Annie. Yes, she was as well as could be expected, and she still visited. In fact that was the reason for her letter. On her last visit Annie had shown her a newspaper clipping, and with me in mind she had asked to borrow it. Going to the sideboard she produced a folded piece of newsprint, with a section marked by a cross, top and bottom, and a photograph attached.

Cut from an American weekly newspaper, published in a town I had never heard of, and the state not mentioned, it had been given to Annie by a local family after a visit to the States.

"What do you make of that?" she asked me. "Does that photo remind you of anyone?"

"No one I can think of," I replied.

"Not Annie's husband?" she questioned.

"Well I don't know, I only saw him once or twice," I said. "He was clean-shaven then, you can't really tell behind that beard, but I suppose there is a resemblance if you search for it."

She interrupted, "Read the cutting, I'd be interested to know what you think and so would Annie, not that she'd do anything about it. It's all 'Water Under the Bridge' now. But it would be nice to know one way or the other, and set her mind at rest."

And this is, as I copied it, the contents of the piece of newsprint:

"The citizens of Millbank are somewhat disturbed and curious at the continued absence of our much respected Rev. R. Williamson, Pastor of our local non-conformist chapel and brotherhood, from a somewhat obscure background. He arrived here several years ago, and charmed us all with his drive and eloquence. Under his guidance the chapel grew and prospered, the congregation increased three-fold, as he introduced new methods of Worship, particularly appealing to the younger members. In fact plans were a-foot to rebuild and add a large additional structure to the original building in answer to the appeal by the Rev. gentleman to the citizens of this town, and who responded magnificently to his call. His work over the years placed considerable strain in his health, so it was with our blessing, we agreed he should have a month's vacation on the coast before work started on the project. He left with the good wishes of us all. It is now six weeks, and no word or message has been received from him, and local members of the chapel, particularly those concerned with the finances of the building fund, are getting more and more apprehensive that something unforeseen may have happened to cause his absence. Police have been notified but unfortunately they have little jurisdiction outside the boundaries of our own state. We can only hope for his safe and speedy return."

I laid down the scrap of paper.

"Well?" she said.

I thought for a moment before replying.

"It may be coincidence, which is unlikely, but all it seems to prove is 'The Lord helps those who help themselves'."

And we left it at that.

7

The Postman Calls

It was early spring, around 1925, that I first met Mr. Jonathan. I was patching up my dinghy, a perpetual and recurring chore, but a free gift and not to be despised. I was aware of a stranger watching me with considerable interest. He was middle aged, fifty or so, of medium height, dark, with a drooping moustache and bushy eyebrows, and the complexion of an outdoor man. A Norfolk jacket, knee length trousers, black leather gaiters and big black boots completed the picture. I was always ready to talk: I am one of those fortunate beings that can talk and still work at the same time. He passed the time of day, and came straight to the point.

"Could I sell him a boat?" What sort or kind of boat had he in mind, I asked. "Like those out there," he replied, pointing to the sea. "Out there" were dozens of boats, all shapes and sizes, yachts, bawleys, barges, even steamers, so this wasn't particularly helpful. I tried again; could he see one about the size he wanted? He pointed to a large yacht, "The Osprey", about 25ft long, and by a strange coincidence she actually was on the market, if not officially for sale. Yes, he could have that one or something like it for about £80. The shocked look on his face was quite sufficient to show me that my commission on that sale would never be. He then mentioned a sum of £20; what could he buy for that? I pointed out a fairly old, beamy seventeen footer, with a short mast, and complete with sails, which had lain all winter off the beach just opposite the minstrels' hut and adjoining our beach. I told him it was in good condition and safe. With a good scrub, tarring and painting there were still many years of useful life left in her. I agreed that I could do all this for him at very little cost and an understanding was reached.

At this point I began to notice a curious agitation in him; his face began to twitch and his eyes didn't seem quite normal. But he produced five one pound notes from his pocket and, taking me literally at my face value, in spite of the fact he had never seen me before and I could have been anybody patching an old boat on the

foreshore, he handed them over. He asked me to enter into nego-
tiations immediately to buy the boat I had pointed out. Actually I
was in no way even sure the owner of the boat in question was
wishful to sell, but as he rarely used it and sadly neglected its
upkeep, I thought there was every chance of his parting with it,
which eventually was the case.

Having received the deposit on that condition, and that he was
genuine in his desire to own a boat, I thought it advisable to find
out just how much he knew about boats and sailing, as quite obviously by his approach he knew very little. I questioned carefully –
was he sure he wanted a boat, and had he been on the water previously? Did he realize that although the sea was calm today, it
could at times be very dangerous even in these sheltered waters?
At each question his face twitched more and more. He seemed to
be growing angrier and angrier, and then burst out:

"If I want to buy a bl***y boat and drown my bl***y self that's
my bl***y business." And then it came pouring out in a stream of
foul language, his troubles at home, his unfaithful wife, his col-
leagues at work, the town council, the police, everyone was against
him. Now I was trying to stop him having what he had always
wanted, a boat. After a while, as suddenly as it started, he calmed
down, the twitch stopped and he was normal again. I was trying to
explain I had only his interests at heart and that my questioning
was purely to safeguard him from the dangers inherent in owning
a small boat. His mood changed and he became quite pleasant,
much to my relief. Then, without even a receipt for his money, and
telling me he would come and see me again in about a fortnight,
and hoping I would be able to buy the boat mentioned, he said he
must now be off to catch his train back to London.

This, I think, was one of the strangest sales of a boat I ever
made. He never even inspected it, or looked at it closely. He had
no idea of what he wanted in a boat, or what was entailed in its
equipment or upkeep, or the simplest requirements in its routine
maintenance. He hadn't even asked about mooring fees or rights,
and owing to his sudden outburst, I had forgotten to tell him.

But with an eye on the 5% commission, which was quite a useful sum in those days, I lost no time in contacting the owner, who
lived in The Ridgeway quite near by. It was soon agreed that he
would accept the £20, which seemed the sum my client had set,

irrespective of bargaining, which was generally and normally the case.

I awaited with curiosity and some doubts my next meeting, and also realized I didn't even know my client's name for a receipt for the final amount. In the meantime he had taken me on trust, so to reciprocate that trust I got the boat out of the water, scrubbed a winter's growth of weed and barnacles off the bottom, gave it a coat of tar, and cleaned and repainted the topsides, inside, seats and thwarts, checked sails and gear, and it was soon a tidy, ship-shape little craft, awaiting its new owner.

He appeared a fortnight to the day. He was delighted; his face lit up with joy like a child with a new toy. He sat in it, pulled the sails up and down under my directions, and to satisfy myself I asked him to do it again on his own. Somehow he just couldn't quite get the hang of it and when the hoist got jammed in the block at the masthead, once again I was treated to a show of anger, bad language and facial contortions like my previous experience. Then again he slowly calmed down and having put this little trouble right he was once again quite normal, but made no attempt to apologise. He handed over the outstanding purchase price, paid me for my work and thanked me for what I had done. I learned his name and he was off to catch his train back to London, but also with the added knowledge that he worked in the Post Office and had to be on shift.

This was all I ever learned of his occupation or where he lived. But I little realized how much of his private life I had to endure every time he arrived and departed with regularity during the following summer months. I began to dread his arrival, and whenever possible avoided him. Fortunately his little boat was now on its moorings, but when the tide was in it was necessary to ferry him to it in my dinghy, or if the tide was out he would come and seek me out. He would almost physically pin me down and subject me to long and obscene stories of his wife's infidelities, of the men, mostly his workmates, lurking in the shadows waiting for him to go out or, when he was at work, how the local council and various councillors were all combined to rob him of his home. Other times it was the turn of the electricity or gas companies that were the objects of his hate; neighbours on both sides were lined up against him and were in league with his wife to poison him and the police were forever watching him, only awaiting the opportunity to imprison him. All this I had to endure with its accompanying bad language and much facial twitching, while his drooping moustache wobbled in sympathy and his face deepened to a dark red hue.

During this time I was usually edging him slowly either towards my dinghy if the tide was in, or if the tide was out gradually work down the beach and onto the mud where he would walk, irrespective that he had boots on, to his boat. Once aboard he would sit very quietly for quite a long time and then suddenly get up, wave his arms about and swear loudly, much to the amazement of any swimmers around, of whom there were many, as the boat was still moored on its original mooring just off the beach.

But for the most part he sat quietly gazing out to sea, watching the beach or eating the sandwiches he brought in a little tin box. As far as I know he never read a book, hoisted the sails or left the moorings, and I strongly suspect he could not row. It was plain to me that this was his only way of getting some peace and rest from his tortured and unsettled mind. Here he was away from all the daily happenings and disturbances of the world, which was against him and determined to destroy him. Fortunately, for some reason I am glad to say he did not count me among them – perhaps because I had no connection with his home affairs – but I lived in fear that I might incur his anger and trod very softly when dealing with him. It was quite plain that he was mentally disturbed and I was surprised that he was still allowed to continue living in society. I think it speaks well for the amazing tolerance of his wife and those in daily contact with him.

The only occasion I saw him actually violent was on his usual visit when he found some children playing in his boat. On ordering them out they were cheeky to him, and he promptly pushed them over in the mud. The father of the children sitting on the beach saw it happening and was off across the mud to the scene of the disturbance, and in no time a right royal battle commenced surrounded by a group of cheering and excited children. To the cheers of the crowd they rolled in the mud and were an unbelievable sight, caked in mud from head to foot. The police were called and they fared little better trying to separate them, but eventually both combatants were taken off in the familiar blue van.

How he got home I don't know and I never asked, but it would seem that even in the one peaceful place he had found he was being persecuted by those around him after this, and no Court proceedings followed. He usually arranged his visit when the tide was in, so peace was resumed. I suggested he might like to change his moorings away from the beach but no, in some queer way, while he thought the world was against him, from his vantage point on the boat he enjoyed watching that same world, but detached from it by a strip of water.

As the autumn came and the weather grew colder his visits grew less and on his last visit towards the end of October he asked me to bring the boat up and store it for the winter. He thanked me most profusely, almost embarrassingly, for looking after him, as he called it, and hoped to see me in early spring, something I was not quite sure I looked forward particularly to. But about the January following I had a letter from a firm of solicitors. It went something like this:

Dear Sir,

We understand you have a yacht in your charge the property of Mr. J Jonathan of 170 ****** Street, Woodford, London. This yacht is now for sale and any offer for the same must be submitted to the above address within a month.

> We are, dear Sir,
> Yours obediently,
> Makepeace & Makepeace.

I wrote telling them that far from being a yacht, the boat in question was a large sailing dinghy, at least twenty years old, and was sold to Mr. Jonathan for £20 the previous year. I was prepared to buy it personally for £15 or offer it for sale at £20, but pointed out that it was a bad time of the year to find customers. My offer was accepted shortly after and it became my property until I disposed of it, redecorated, later that spring. Having the impression that solicitors never disclosed their clients' affairs I thought it improper to ask what had happened to Mr. Jonathan, and felt perhaps it would be wrong to write to the address mentioned, so to this day fifty years later I still don't know the complete end to this story. But I would be dishonest if I did not admit I was greatly relieved, and this brings to mind the sequel . . . in the next story.

48

8

The Builder
or, let dogs delight . . .

The boat was purchased from me by a young medical student, to my relief a very normal young man, who very soon learnt to sail and spent most of his time that summer enjoying his newly acquired boat. He was always accompanied by his dog, an English terrier, whose only fault was a determined desire to fight, however large, any or every dog in sight. That he enjoyed the sea as much as his master was self-evident, and immediately on seeing the dinghy, the ferry to his master's boat, he would rush down the beach at breakneck speed, and take a flying leap, sometimes across a gap of water some four or five feet across, when it was moored some little distance from the water's edge. It would rush back and forth in it barking furiously the while, until his master arrived, and again the same performance at the other end when we arrived at jumping distance.

Sometimes the young student would bring his books and study in the peace and restfulness of the mooring, and one day I was surprised to see among them a book with a title something like "Home Improvements & Alterations for the Beginner". When I remarked on it I was informed that both he and his neighbour's life had become a perpetual nightmare through their dogs. The big Airedale owned by his neighbour and his dog were sworn enemies and constantly at each other's throats through the dividing fence of his home. It is certain that neither dog would have given in and highly probable that one would be torn to pieces – more than likely the terrier – so they had decided to build a high brick wall, right down the dividing line of their properties, the neighbour to supply the bricks and he to do the work.

So with that in mind he had bought the book to learn bricklaying, and how to go about it. He thought perhaps later he might possibly add the long-wanted addition to his mother's home. I was

49

interested and usually enquired how his efforts were progressing, and to my surprise in a comparatively short time it was completed and he was applying for building permission for the extension that he had spoken of. The summer ended and I saw nothing of him until the following spring, when he turned up one day complete with dog and full of enthusiasm. He had given up his medical career, and was now building houses, apparently very successfully.

He had moved his boat to moorings at Benfleet and I saw nothing more of him for some long time, when he again visited me, bigger and heavier, expensively dressed and quite plainly very prosperous, this time accompanied by a huge Labrador. I was delighted to see him, and I think he was equally pleased, but somehow he was not his old blithe happy self. The youth and spirit were gone. He was tired and tense; he offered me a cigar. I refused. He said:

"Wish I could. I smoke too much."

Was he still building? I asked. Yes, he had a very large estate in progress. How about a boat? Yes, a large yacht, The Enchantress. I had seen, and envied her. But he had so little time to use it. But, he added, almost with an apologetic look, he could see it from the house – he didn't call it "home", but that might have been just an omission – that he had just completed overlooking the sea. We talked of the old days and I had the feeling he would have gladly parted with his present material blessings to bring them back. But with his present commitments, deep involvements, a growing and expensive family, in no way could he turn back the clock, and in no way was the rat race or society going to release him.

I didn't see him again, but his name cropped up from time to time in the local papers, as he became more wealthy and more prominent in the public eye. "J.P." and later "O.B.E." were added to his name, and his death while still a comparatively young man was well publicised and the success story that followed filled quite half of the front page of a well known local paper.

Not an unusual or even an original story, and the usual predictable ending, and my only excuse for even putting it in print was its connection with the little boat mentioned in my earlier story. Or maybe because I was involved to some small degree with someone who became the envy or inspiration of those who seek material gain. Or was it just a touch of guilt that I hadn't or couldn't do the same? I don't think so; on second thoughts I think it is just the amazing end results, in the right setting, of two dogs fighting through a fence.

9

The Yachtsman who Never Sailed

(Alternative titles: 'The Armchair Sailor',
or 'The Sailor Who lived in the Past')

It was about this period, or maybe a little later, that Mr. Lynch came into my life. He was introduced to me by one of my regular customers; he informed me that Mr. Lynch was a recently joined member of the local Yacht Club, was having a boat built by Cole & Wiggins in Leigh, and could I find him a mooring and look after him, a strange request considering he was perhaps nearly three times my age, but I realized how it was meant, and promised he would be duly cared for.

My subsequent memories always in some vague and indefinite way reminded me of Mr. Jonathan. Yet in no possible way, other, perhaps than just sitting in their boats, was there any characteristic, either physical or mental, resemblance between them. Mr. Lynch was always a pleasure to see and talk with; he was an intelligent and interesting man, and I welcomed his visits. He was a small, round man with a head, bald except for a fringe of long, greyish-white hair that seemed to be on the wrong body, surmounted by a large, new yachting cap, sporting the Leigh Sailing Club badge, and dressed in a dark blue suit of semi-naval or nautical cut.

But he looked less a sailor and much more a pixie or gnome, bulging eyes and a moulded putty nose of no particular shape, and a pipe that seemed part of his mouth. Not a flattering description, but an overall happiness that was catching to all who came in contact with him. I was also puzzled by his skin. Maybe this was why I thought of pixies; it was completely hairless and had the pink and white appearance that follows severe burns. Here and there were eruptions and semi-healed sores quite pitiful to look at. His hands,

I was horrified to see, were twisted and misshapen; the fingers with no nails looked as though they had been crushed in a machine and the complete hand and wrist had the appearance of just recovering from being immersed in boiling water or liquid.

I must admit I was intensely shocked, but also curious, but felt at this early stage I had no right to pry into such a personal suffering, and far better ignored, and I behaved as though I had never noticed. But I learned afterwards that he had been one of a team of doctor scientists involved in the early experiments with X-rays, and the results of direct contact with these dangerous rays. He had paid dearly in his efforts to help humanity, and I am afraid received little gratitude in return. But never once did he complain or refer to this part of his life, and I respected his silence.

Having no moorings available I suggested applying for permission, and I would sink the necessary root and supply the chain etc. some hundred yards from the beach, where I could keep an eye on his new boat, which he had spent many hours in designing and was now almost finished and ready to sail. I had seen previous efforts in amateur boat designing over the years; some works of art, others dangerous and unseaworthy, all built by enthusiastic, but in most cases quite impractical people. A few outstanding examples gave their owners many years of enjoyment and even won races, and one of these, "Strong Mac" built by a Mr. Naughton, was an outstanding success and raced for many years with the Leigh Sailing Club, and is remembered by many.

I waited with interest to see this combination of amateur designing and professional boat building. When shortly after our first meeting, and within days of fixing the mooring, Mr. Lynch arrived with his wife to welcome the results of the combined effort, I was nearly as excited as he was. But Mrs. Lynch, a small, grey haired, bespectacled, rather stern faced, no nonsense person, showed no trace of agitation or excitement so apparent in her husband. She sat down in a deck chair, produced her knitting from a large bag and proceeded calmly, with an occasional "Don't fuss, George" or "Be quiet, George" to knit steadily while he searched, restlessly, the distance in the direction of Old Leigh. And true to their promise the boat eventually arrived in charge of a Leigh fisherman to be installed on its new mooring. But first it landed on the beach.

53

Contrary to my fears, it was beautifully designed. Beamy and with lovely lines, it seemed to have twice the room of the normal seventeen footer. Beautifully built with its elm planking and mahogany thwarts and seats, it shone in varnished splendour and the copper nails gleamed in the sunlight. Here was a creation anyone could envy; it was just such a boat that I had pictured in my own dreams and here in actual fact it was, and I must admit I really wished it was my own. We tried hoisting and lowering the lovely white cotton sails supplied by that expert of Leigh sailmakers, Francy Tunnidge, as he was fondly called by the Leigh men. The brightly varnished mast and spars were a joy to look at and handle, and my opinion of the designer increased even more and I congratulated him enthusiastically, much to his added joy, on the success of his efforts.

During all this excitement Mrs. Lynch calmly continued her knitting, occasionally smiling in the same way that mothers have when their children have found a plaything that keeps them quiet. But never once did the needles stop clicking and during that summer, when she arrived with her husband to visit his boat, the procedure never changed. But rarely, very rarely, she talked to my mother, and there emerged a person who cared very deeply and greatly admired this little man, her husband. Her sole concern was his happiness, albeit more perhaps as a mother, and he her grown-up son. The boat duly admired, it was taken to its moorings and was soon sitting on the mud, the excitement of the great day over.

A few days later they again turned up. Mrs. Lynch promptly settled in her deck chair and the clicking of needles continued. Mr. Lynch couldn't wait to get to his boat. It was a glorious day and as soon as there was sufficient water I ferried him across and put him aboard, both of us singing her praises and admiring her beauty. Soon I saw the sails go up, and he seated at the helm going through the motions of sailing. But the sails hung limply with not a breath of wind and he had not let go the moorings. Nothing was happening. In a little while he lowered the sails, stowed them neatly, and busied himself mopping floorboards and other activities I couldn't see, and then sat for the rest of the tide in much the same way as Mr. Jonathan had done previously. But he came ashore at the end of the tide full of praise and delightfully happy with his new possession.

He and Mrs. Lynch became regular visitors every warm summer day, although if I remember rightly there were few that year, she with her bag of knitting, and he with bits of matchboarding and toolbag. He still pulled up the sails on very calm days, then lowered them, but now most of his time was occupied with building lockers under the rear seats, and other small jobs, or again just sitting in it enjoying the calls of the gulls or perhaps the lopping waters against her bilges.

At no time did Mrs. Lynch ever lose patience or ever show any signs of resentment at these long sessions aboard, and my admiration grew the longer I knew her. Once or twice he hoisted and set his sails straight away on boarding and I thought, he really is going for a sail today. But no, down they came after a little while and then back to his normal routine. Then suddenly I realized, almost with unbelief, the truth. *He couldn't sail* and was frightened to try and equally frightened to admit it, to either himself or others. He knew all about the construction, navigation, which at odd times he was teaching me, knew all the nautical terms of both gear and rigging. In fact from many years of study he knew all about boats, but when it came to the actual sailing of his boat he had no practical experience whatsoever.

Whether it was fear of others knowing, fear of putting into practice all his theoretical knowledge, or just that he had all his ambitions satisfied in seeing his dreams in reality, I don't know, and I had no intention of letting him know I knew. So one day I suggested that I would dearly love to sail her and with a moment's hesitation he agreed. Overboard went the mooring buoy for the first time and we were away. She sailed like a witch – lived up to every hope her beauty promised, clawed to windward with centre-board down like a racing boat. I suggested to him that he took the helm, although loath to give it up. I passed the tiller to him and I realized almost immediately that I had been right in my surmise and that he had never actually sailed a boat in his life. Without appearing to notice, I handed him the main sheet and suggested that perhaps as a new boat she might want getting a little used to and that it was naturally a little difficult that one had not previously sailed in.

He gratefully accepted this, and very quickly handed back both tiller and sheet, saying that as I was enjoying it so much it was a pity for me not to continue sailing it. We had one of the most enjoyable sails that day I ever remember, and not the least of this the pleasure it gave him to see all his hopes fulfilled, and his designing, completely and absolutely perfect. But I do, even now, wonder just how much Cole & Wiggins added or subtracted to the original design, in its building, to produce such a perfect little gem.

I went with him several times that summer and tried hard to make him sail it but always after a few minutes he seemed to panic and passed it back, saying he enjoyed it equally if not better as a passenger, and would have a turn later, and I admit that this arrangement suited me as she was one of the finest little craft I ever handled. He still never left the moorings on his own but was as happy as the day was long doing his little carpentry jobs etc., and a very shipshape job he made of it all, no mean feat when one considered his misshapen hands and perhaps the pain that went with them.

I was really sorry when the season ended and his boat was taken away for winter storage. Whether he suspected I knew his secret I don't quite know. Certainly no one at the Yacht Club had any doubts as to his ability to sail. He had been seen out sailing several times; that someone else was with him for company was natural, and he was in great demand for hints in design. I never mentioned a word to anyone; I liked him too much to hurt him, he had been hurt enough in his life, and so the charade continued.

The following spring it was back, resplendent with bright varnish and shining spars, the results of much loving labour, considering he was now getting on in years, and his other physical handicaps, and the situation settled back into its previous routine; the clicking of needles went on much as before, the only difference being the colour of the wool.

I endeavoured to take him for an occasional sail, but my business was growing, and least of all could I spare the time when the tide was in.

But the problem solved itself. One of my dinghy boys, a lad of fifteen, an extremely sensible and reliable boy, had during the winter built himself a small flat-bottomed sailing dinghy, not a craftsman's job by any stretch of the imagination, but it was water-tight and safe. With the cut-off top of an old mainsail, it sailed surprisingly well, and in a very little while he had learned to sail quite efficiently.

One day I was about to take Mr. Lynch out sailing, when I suggested taking this youngster with us. He agreed and in no time a bond arose between them. The boy's father had never been interested. Mr. Lynch had never had a son, and from then on the problem was solved; they became the greatest of friends and many happy hours they spent together. But it was always the youth who sailed the boat, its owner never having either the will or desire to try to learn.

This state of affairs continued for several summers, until the young man went overseas and the owner grew too old to really enjoy it. But he never learnt to sail. For all intents and purposes this should have made a nice complete and satisfactory end to an interesting and pleasant recollection. But it was not to be.

Our paths crossed again, some three or four years later; he showed me another facet of his character which I am sure very few others had witnessed or would have believed. It left me completely bewildered and only by actually seeing the occurrence do I really know it took place. These are the facts; I leave it to those who read this to draw their own conclusions.

A small query over a navigational problem had arisen between myself and a friend which could not be easily resolved and almost immediately my thoughts flew to Mr. Lynch. If anyone knew the answer he most likely would. I knew he was still around, through members of the Leigh Sailing Club. So shortly afterwards I took the liberty of calling on him. Both he and Mrs. Lynch made me very welcome, and over a cup of coffee in his study, surrounded by the most impressive array of technical books short of a library, my query was answered and, what was more, I was wrong. But this in no way altered the pleasure of his society, and when he invited me to see some of his model ships that he was busily engaged in making, I jumped at the chance, as I had earlier been a keen maker of ship models myself.

He led me down his garden to a small shed mostly occupied by a large bench. His tools all neatly arrayed on shelves were typical of his ordered way of life. At the far end was a lovely model of his own little boat. A Thames sailing barge, a Leigh cockle boat and a bawley occupied other shelves, but pride of place was taken by a fine model of a full rigged ship much the same as the famous "Cutty Sark".

As I had myself some knowledge of this type of ship, from my own model making, we discussed the technicalities of handling such a ship at sea and I was amazed at his knowledge. As he continued to describe life at sea on such a vessel he became more and more excited and agitated in his speech, and started pacing back and forth behind his bench, much as though he was walking the quarter deck of a fine ship. Suddenly he became transformed, he seemed to grow taller, his voice deep and forceful, and in front of me he became master of this ship whose model stood in front of us. The orders, loud and clear in the salty language of the day, poured out, and I realized it was his intention to bring this vessel about and alter course on the other tack. Occasionally glancing over his shoulder, he gave instructions to an invisible man at the wheel.

How completely accurate the orders and complete operation were I don't know, but everything sounded exactly as if it was really happening, and for that moment in time I stood with him looking into the waist of that fine ship. The rhythmic pull on ropes and halyards as each order rang out, repeated by the leaders of the crews as they hauled or lowered the sails to the commands. Men in the rigging and along the footropes of the huge spars as they swung in the new course, the rattle of blocks, the sails shivering, emptying, and slowly, very slowly filling, the lean from upright of the masts, the sails pulling as she gathered way on her new course. It was as if for a moment he had carried me into another place and age with him, because there is little doubt in my mind he was, for that little while, that ship's master. He was not acting, unless he was the most gifted of actors, and as he slowly gave his last order and once again became his normal self he didn't even seem to know of the interlude, and continued with his conversation as though it had never happened.

Had he intended it, surely he would have prepared me in some way by mentioning what he was about to do. In retrospect I think it more likely that during quiet hours of making this model, he became a complete part of it, and totally immersed. By this love of the sea and ships, his conversation with me for the first time with a technical knowledge and a kindred spirit, had sparked off a type of self-hypnotism or some such physiological effect peculiar to the situation.

Or possibly there is another explanation, something I hesitate to suggest or pass judgement on – the theory of reincarnation. Is it just possible that the circumstances being right, he lived for that short time a previous existence as a sailor, a man of the sea? His love of the sea was deeply ingrained in his whole being, there is little doubt. I am not qualified to pass judgement; all I do know was that it leaves room for thought, and was an extremely interesting experience. I never saw him again; I regret it now but with the thoughtlessness of youth and my days so full I never found time to call again. I was always going to. Later a little note from Mrs. Lynch informed me that Mr. Lynch had passed on: a finish to my story, but no satisfactory answer to my queries.

10

The Captain's Reprieve

"To those who go down to the sea in ships,
and have their business on the great waters"

What a lovely prayer, and what pictures it conjures up in the mind, the harbours of the world, the new world of commerce and travel, a forest of masts and spars and white sails drying in the sunshine. Human cargoes, spices from the East, everything that ships can carry, and men of all nations bonded by "their business on the great waters".

Such a man was Captain Woods. I noticed him several times as he looked at the boats I had charge of during the winter months. I was always aware of a stranger; there were no holiday-makers and only a few locals around, and he looked an interesting character. Of medium height, broad of shoulder, weather beaten, with a finely trimmed beard, he looked what he was, a real sailorman, with a yachting cap quite unlike those so favoured by our local yachtsmen. Perhaps it would be more correct to call it a Captain's hat. The gold badge of a shipping line, prominently displayed, a faded blue suit of the type only sailor men's shops supply, double breasted, gold buttons and braid, advertised plainly that here was a real man of the sea, and as always I was ready for a chat. I wished him good morning and in no time we were established friends. We talked of the sea and ships.

A kindly, gentle man, he was not a bit like the ranting blustering skipper we read about in books, yet he had been one. Apprenticed in sail at an early age he had sailed the seven seas, been in most harbours of the world, sailed around The Horn in the storms of winter. I had never previously met such a man, yet it was all told quietly and with no attempt to impress or glorify. It was more my questioning that brought to light the treasure house of his recollections and adventures. He had decided he would like to buy a small sailing boat, and should I hear of one, let him know, and he handed me his card – "Captain Woods", and underneath

"Deep Sea Pilot", and then his address. It was the beginning of a friendship I look back on with pleasure.

Several days later he again appeared and this time came immediately to see me. I seated him on my special beer crate reserved only for those I really liked and he informed me that he had just returned from Rotterdam, and produced from his pocket a large slab of dark unsweetened Dutch chocolate which he gave me. It was then that I learned he was still actively engaged in piloting ships across the North Sea, although to me he seemed well beyond retirement age. It showed in his tired eyes straining into winter darkness in all weathers and conditions, but otherwise he was a fine fit man.

Every several days he left his home in Leigh and travelled to London by train and thence to Middlesbrough; there he took command of one of a number of ships belonging to a Japanese shipping line – The Nippon Yusan Kiasha Shipping Firm – which he would pilot either to Rotterdam or Amsterdam, pick up another of the same line and bring it back with cargo to Middlesbrough Docks, home again to Leigh for a few days and off again across the North Sea.

It was for those few days at home he wanted to do a little sailing, a strange and unusual method of relaxation when one already spent most of the time at sea. I can only think that perhaps like a nagging wife, when she wasn't there, he missed her. I now had a boat, sixteen footer, old but sound, gaff rigged and roomy lined up for him, but had not proceeded further until he himself could pass judgement on its suitability. It was going cheap and he decided then and there to buy it and later it proved to be just what he wanted, and many were the happy hours he spent sailing or just pottering around in it.

He had married late in life, and he seldom spoke of his personal life. His wife, a previous school mistress, was much younger and I gathered had little use for the sea, and I never remember her ever setting foot on his boat. They had one son about fourteen of whom he was extremely proud. Even more so when, on entering a nationwide competition by a national newspaper to find the most brilliant boy in Britain, he won it. He later achieved even greater triumphs, but he showed not the slightest interest in his father's love of the sea or small boat sailing. He was his mother's boy.

Our friendship continued, and as always on his return a welcome awaited him on my beer crate which now, by the way, was upholstered with sail cloth and an impressive array of brass-headed nails and even more selective of those that were allowed to sit on it. I received my slab of Dutch chocolate, which by now was standard practice, and which I was almost beginning to enjoy, and this I repaid by looking after his boat while away on his voyages. What was more, my mother, who was in command during the summer, approved completely, which was not always the case with the motley crowd of all ages that drifted around through the mass unemployment of that period, and I at different times collected. I knew she approved by the frequent cups of tea that passed out of the window of our shed, and which like my beer crate were only for the selected few.

As usual our talks were mostly of the sea, but he was a well read man and we covered many things, "of shoes and ships and sealing wax and cabbages and kings." But it nearly always came back to ships and the men that sailed them. He mentioned many famous vessels; some he had even been aboard. Quite often at that time many fine schooners, barges and barquentines and even full-rigged ships were still passing or being towed up and down among the steamers in the Thames. They often sparked off another story, but mostly they had to be coaxed out of him. And my deep regret at not recording these stories at the time will remain with me all my life. But I was young and with the thoughtlessness of youth, lived with little thought of the values of the future or keeping note of time.

This happy state of affairs continued for at least three or more years but the strain was beginning to show on him. He was getting tired and noticeably not well. He mentioned the ship's doctor had given him a letter to a specialist in London. I feared the worst. This was confirmed a few days later when he kept the appointment; it was that dreaded of all diseases – cancer – and with luck six months of life left.

He took the blow fate had dealt him calmly and with dignity, informed me that he had given in his notice to the company, and intended to spend what was left of his life on and around his little boat, and all through that summer he did just that. Mother was even more kind to him and even added biscuits to his cup of tea, an honour indeed! He dismissed all thoughts of illness, and fortunately did not suffer severe pain.

Six months came and went, then nine months, and our fears gave way to hope. Slowly but surely his health began to improve, and the specialist's forecast was questioned and eventually proved wrong. And he was still very much alive and well the following year, when he decided the boat and the journey to the beach was getting a little too much for him, leaving both my mother and I very sure that no one like him would again sit on my beer crate.

But the story did not end there. Quite a number of years after, and when I had left the beach, I was working on a bungalow in Grassmead Avenue and got chatting with an elderly grey-haired lady in the bungalow at the bottom of the garden. To my surprise I found that she was housekeeper to Captain Woods, now a very old man, and there was no doubt he was my Captain Woods.

She offered to let me see him, warning me that he was bedridden, had had a stroke and didn't recognise anyone. To my shame I just could not bring myself to see him like this, for a man I had so much respect and even perhaps affection. I couldn't face it. I wanted to remember him as he used to be and the man we knew. I made an excuse, said perhaps tomorrow, and never saw him.

He must have been very old, and perhaps this story will bring some little hope and comfort to those who need it, and that even specialists are only human and can be wrong, and our lives and destinies in the hands of a Higher Power.

11

I Go into Films

I suppose that among the more enjoyable aspects of my life on the beach was, unlike the normal and average job, that one never quite knew what fresh faces or events would arise. While life on the average followed a reasonably set pattern, the likelihood of meeting someone or something different was far more likely to occur, as the panorama of life passed along the cinder path and the more recent Westcliff Promenade.

The memory of one of these occasions remains among the many others. It was my first and only introduction into the film world.

It was a lovely day in the height of summer. A stranger walked towards the shed dressed very much like the gangsters and bootleggers depicted on the films so prevalent at that time in the cinemas. He was followed by a motley crowd of similar film-like characters and particularly a strikingly beautiful girl. I was of the age to appreciate her charms and by her dress she also realized it. Luxurious dark hair in coils almost to her waist. Only the excessive quantity of make-up on face and lips spoilt her perfection and beauty to a degree.

The leader approached mother, who I could see immediately disapproved of the young lady and most of the others, but after a few minutes of conversation he seemed to charm her into a different frame of mind, as I found out later, by telling her how he had been especially recommended by theatrical friends and how they had assured him of her helpful reputation and even fame in London. How much of this she believed I don't know, I think not much, but it evidently pacified her and she called me over and passed our visitor on to me.

With a theatrical flourish and extended hand he proudly announced his name, at the same time offering me a card bearing the name, if I remember rightly, "Central" or "Century Films Incorporated" and a London address. While I wasn't particularly impressed by this, I confess the young lady had had much the same effect on me as her companion had made on mother, and I was more than ready to be her willing slave.

They explained they wished to shoot a scene in which a castaway, the young lady – and he indicated the siren present – at last after fearful adventures arrives in dire distress, etc. on the shore of a desert island, namely our beach.

As there is a singular absence of suitable palm trees, the background full of bathers and small boots and little, if any surf or coconuts, I pointed out that I doubted if it would look particularly authentic. To this he replied, "The public will believe anything they see on films," and requested a sailing boat and a tent for changing in. The tent was easily supplied; the sailing boat more difficult. I didn't own one myself at that time and those I could have borrowed I would not, without permission, and that took time.

But I was determined to show the heroine that she was not unappreciated and her beauty not overlooked, and I would do all I could to help. My old dinghy was all that I could offer, but it was welcomed as just right and suitably dilapidated for the part. With mounting enthusiasm I suggested supplying a mast and sail, an old oar tied and nailed upright to the front seat, another oar with a sheet or old tent canvas nailed along it and fastened to the top of the upright oar, and a remarkable looking craft came into being. Apart from the fact that it was most unlikely to have survived in any storm, it looked the part far better than any craft I could have borrowed.

By this time the single camera was in position and various technicians were at work. Shortly afterwards a vision in a tattered skirt torn in all the right places, and a blouse that revealed far more than it concealed, emerged from the tent and was suitably installed, lying in apparent exhaustion across the back seat.

The problem then arose, how to take the dinghy approaching from the distance under sail to the shore. I could not appear in the picture, and yet it needed to be controlled, coming ashore with the wind behind it and finding its destination and way to its coral strand without guidance.

Fortunately the very light breeze was exactly right and nothing was going to stop me now. I was prepared to almost lay down my life for the raven haired beauty, that had so suddenly appeared, and so unlike any girl I had ever met. So I rowed out some fifty yards from the shore, at the same time requesting the bathers to leave the vicinity. In any case most had joined the ever increasing crowd gathered on the prom, breakwater or beach.

Once again my passenger arranged herself in the agreed position, and turning the dinghy's bow towards the shore, where a Robinson Crusoe-like figure was pacing back and forth, I slipped overboard in shirt and trousers and with the sail gently filling acted as a rudder. Holding the keel at the stern, and completely out of sight, with camera operating, I headed to the beach.

It was unfortunate that having picked up the rescued and forlorn "castaway" in his arms he tripped and, to the cheers of the crowd, dropped her into the water and fell on top of her. This made it necessary for the whole performance to be recorded again. The second time everything went successfully. And that it seemed, was all they wanted.

Packing up their gear, changing back into their normal clothes, and with a promise of information and free tickets when it was completed, they left. Having heard of the lavish methods and payments made by film companies, I had tentatively speculated in my mind what my reward would be. Nothing extravagant, of course, maybe a pound, perhaps even more. I had spent most of the afternoon, and quite a bit of work, in fixing things. When time to settle for the use of the tent came, I was prepared to say, "I'll leave it to you," which I thought was fair.

As it was, with a hurried "thank you", a smile from the "castaway", they left as they had arrived out of nowhere, back to obscurity. I never heard of either the film or the players afterwards, but perhaps even now in some dusty archive that little bit of "Joscelyne's Beach" and my dinghy in film are lying on a shelf.

And I cannot even claim "I was in a film" – or was I?

12

A Trip to Gravesend (or very nearly)

I cannot recall my first meeting with Mr. Ostermayer. He always just seemed to be around, like a part of the foreshore and not noticed or missed until he wasn't there, which was very rare. Long thin arms and legs and a long thin red face with a noticeably long pointed nose, and long thin fair hair. A beanpole of a man. He seemed in some vague way to remind me of those distorted shapes that one finds in "the hall of mirrors" at the fairgrounds.

He usually wore a battered and dilapidated seaman's peaked cap of a slightly foreign appearance and had possibly adorned the head of some foreign seaman, been washed overboard and had laid among the seaweed and rubbish on the tideline until rescued and given a home. It was particularly noticeable because it was entirely out of keeping with the rest of his attire, which consisted usually of ex-army surplus khaki jacket and trousers, surmounted with an ex-army greatcoat, which he wore to keep out the rain and cold of the winter months and most of the summer to keep out the heat of the sun. A pair of short wellingtons completed his outfit and also gave him the means to cross the mud to his boat.

It must have been after 1918, otherwise the army surplus would not have been available. Whether he had done army service I don't know; he was more than old enough, but I doubt it. He spoke perfect English but was of German extraction. Either his parents or grandparents were of that nationality and I think quite well off, but he never discussed his private affairs. To look at him one would be tempted to hand over a few coppers and suggest he bought something to eat. But actually he was well and wisely provided for, and regularly received a substantial sum every three months from a trust fund provided by his parents after they had died. Consequently he had never actually worked for a living in his life, and that of course accounted for his always being around.

Interfering with no one, he was accepted and well liked in the pubs of Old Leigh among the fishermen, and quietly and unobtrusively mingled with both beachcombers and the customers on "Joscelyne's Beach" and I quite looked forward to his regular visits. When I ferried him out to his boat I never charged him. Neither he nor I expected it.

But when he had a good day's fishing, his main interest, he would hand over a feed of fish all nicely cleaned to Mother, which amply compensated for the small service I provided.

Of his home life he said little. He was married and lived in his own house in Cliff Road. His wife was well built and still retained the looks of a very attractive woman. She looked after him well, as she also did "the lodger", a fine, mature looking man, also of German extraction, who regularly showed his appreciation by taking his landlady on holiday with him. What arrangements existed between them all, I never knew or even wanted to know; I had little interest in such things. But it worried Mother a lot, I think, at the lack of knowledge on this subject. She didn't know if to blame or feel sorry for him, but it seemed to work amicably and with no jealousy.

Time never seemed to hang on his hands but from casual conversation I gathered he was expected to do a lot of the housework and shopping. But immediately he was free of his daily "chores" he would wander into Old Leigh among his friends in the cosy surroundings of The Ship or The Smack, but first and foremost to his boat, a sixteen foot open boat. It was built for him by Cole & Wiggins, who had recently started boat building on Victoria Wharf in Leigh, and before their removal later to more spacious premises beyond the cockle sheds (where Johnson & Jago followed after them).

This boat was his real love; it had a small "Evinrude" outboard motor and was the first outboard I or many others had seen. Most of the smaller boats that had engines were either old converted car engines or made by two local firms – the "Little Demon", a single cylinder 4.h.p. with an enormous flywheel made by the Southend Engineering Co., or the "Leonsie" or 2½.h.p. made a few doors away, both in Leigh High Street (both are still there but no longer make engines). So this outboard was both a curiosity and novelty. With no magneto, it worked from a coil and accumulator, and most of the back seat of his boat was occupied by these and a cob-web of electric wiring. Nearly every day he would bring his fresh-ly charged electrical gear and give the motor a run whether the tide was in or out. He seldom missed a day without running it, and some of the trips he did to the Kent side were almost inviting dis-aster, but he always seemed to manage to get home, usually with a surprisingly large bag of fish. It had been long suggested he had a secret method; whatever it was, it worked and we didn't go short either.

Apart from one failing, or more correctly, weakness, I doubt I should have particularly remembered him, other than one of the many who frequented "Joscelyne's Beach" and Chalkwell fore-shore, except maybe, that eventful trip to Gravesend.

As I previously said, he was in receipt of a substantial sum quarterly and while for the greater part of these twelve weeks he enjoyed his pint or two in his favourite pubs in the Old Town, mostly "on the slate", as he always eventually paid his debts, the first week or so (after settling his previous accounts) it was drinks all round, cigars for a chosen few, and the target of the scroungers that frequented the inns for just such an opportunity. But worse, he didn't know when he himself had "had too much" and for sev-eral days he was far more drunk than sober, and remained so until most of his money was gone.

I have an intense, and perhaps unreasonable hatred of drunk-enness and when he came on the beach in this state I let him know in no uncertain terms he wasn't welcome. To his credit he realized my feelings, bore no ill will and usually kept away.

I well remember the shock I felt when I first had practical expe-rience of his failing. I know, of course, he liked his drink, most everybody along the foreshore did and it was no crime.

It was early in the year, because it was quite cold, and as was my custom, having spent the morning on the beach, I was walking home to dinner along the cinder path. About halfway along I was horrified to see what I thought was the body of Mr. Ostermayer lying on the sea wall a few feet from the footpath. To my relief I found him breathing heavily, his usual red face almost a deep pur-ple, an indication I learnt afterwards was a sure sign, and a deep gash oozing blood on his forehead. There wasn't a soul in sight and every effort to move him proved fruitless. I realized that "dead drunk" was not only an expression but could become a fact.

I just didn't know what to do. I tried to get him on his feet but although he looked so thin, he seemed to weigh a ton and try as I could he wouldn't move. In desperation and anger – and I was strangely angry – I decided to let him stay and sleep it off, consoling my conscience that if he was still there after dinner, on my way back, I would try again.

When I told Mother about it, she was annoyed with me for doing nothing but I don't know what else I could have done at the time. She insisted I had a quick dinner and go back and it was fortunate that I did. I hadn't got far along the cinder path when I was terrified to see Mr. Ostermayer lying at the bottom of the sea wall in the mud. He had apparently rolled or fallen down the wall, and where now the incoming tide was lapping his inert body. He was in a terrible state, cut, bruised and bleeding. He lay on the edge of the tide.

With all my strength I dragged him first feet-first, then head-first and again feet-first, helped fortunately by slippery seaweed, up the slope. To my relief I saw a local fisherman on his way to a little beachcombing approaching. Between us we got him safely onto the cinder path. He was now showing signs of realizing what was happening. Getting him on his feet and supporting him to our beach took a long time but once there I phoned the police from the Grosvenor Tea Rooms and he was taken to hospital and later home. But I am still puzzled how he could have lain there (admitting it was lunch time) without someone seeing him. Did they, like the parable of the Good Samaritan, "pass on the other side", or was the cinder path so little frequented in those far off days?

A couple of days later, a very contrite and sheepish "Osker", as his friends called him (whether this was his Christian name or an abbreviation of his real name I never knew), came to see me. He said how sorry he was, and expressed his regrets at the trouble he had caused me. He brought me a present, a small portable grindstone (which I still have), and I in turn thanked him for his present and in spite of the fact he was so much older, gave him a severe lecture on the evils of alcohol in the possible hope that he would mend his ways. Actually, as time showed it made little or no impression, but I had said my say and we parted the best of friends. And he behaved himself quite well until the next time.

The next time came the following year, much around the same time, cold early spring. He left his boat afloat all through the winter chiefly for the fishing. I used to visit the beach even in winter every day and my dinghy was usually for those few enthusiasts whose boats remained in use during the winter. On this particular day, it was blowing almost a gale from the south west and an exceptionally heavy sea was running, particularly in the triangle formed by our beach and the breakwater, where the backlash was so strong.

A yacht had broken loose from its moorings. With great difficulty I launched my old dinghy and with even greater effort succeeded to get over the heavy breakers pounding the shore, something which after many years I was quite experienced in, and secretly enjoyed. It took little time to board the yacht and lower the anchor and chain and it was soon riding comfortably and safely some fifty yards off the sea wall and cinder path instead of becoming, probably, a total wreck. Once a boat got on "the rocks", as we called the apron wall, there was little hope for it and many a fine boat had been wrecked there.

Returning to the beach it was too rough to land easily, so I cast my anchor overboard about twenty yards off the beach and slowly paid out the cable until the stern was a few feet from the shore and riding "head on" to the waves. Taking advantage of the gap between waves, I scrambled ashore, quite pleased with my morning's work, speculating on how much my services would be generously recognized by the owner of the yacht.

It was getting time to go home to dinner when Osker arrived. I knew by the shade of purple in his face he was intoxicated but not so far gone as to be helpless. Demanding to be put on board his boat, I refused.

He shouted, "Put me aboard my boat."

I again refused, saying, "It's not fit in this weather to go aboard," and added, "You've had too much to drink." He emphatically denied he was the worse for drink. I said he was, but it made no impression and he continued to insist he was sober.

I replied, "I'm getting my dinghy in, and going home to dinner, and you had better do the same." I walked down the beach, awaited a favourable moment and got into the dinghy. The cable was rather tangled and I spent a little time clearing it. I pulled off a few yards and, looking back, to my astonishment and dismay, hanging half over the back seat and trailing his legs in the water was "Osker". Securing the cable, I got to him and pulled him in-board and sat him firmly down. All this time the dinghy was rolling and pitching in the heavy swell, but fortunately riding head on to the waves.

Going for'ard I started once again to haul on the anchor cable and get the dinghy beyond the heavy surf breaking on the beach. In a short while I reached and lifted the anchor, turned swiftly to reach the oars, already in position in their rowlocks so that the boat could be eased backwards, until exactly the right moment between waves allowed me time to "beach" it. Then, to my fear and dismay, I realized I no longer had a passenger; he had gone, vanished.

Suddenly a hand came slowly up out of the water, a yard or two away astern, and the next wave almost carried me past. Looking down into the murky water I saw him lying on his back and waving his arms upwards. I made a grab at his hand and pulled him to the surface. This was no trouble; his body weighed very little in the water, but getting him aboard was a very different matter. His clothes, wellingtons and army great coat made it quite impossible to haul him aboard, and now with me supporting him all on the one side and the dinghy now broadside on to the waves, I was in imminent danger of capsizing. The moment the bilge touched the shore, that was exactly what did happen.

I was thrown out onto the shore and swamped by the next wave, but he was underneath the dinghy somewhere and in even worse danger than previously. How long he was under it I can't remember but with all my strength I lifted it over. The next wave sucked it back on the recoil and I was able to pull his head up out of the surf. Onlookers now came to my aid and we lifted him higher up the beach out of harm's way.

By some remarkable chance he was not seriously injured; the cold water and excitement had by this time sobered him up considerably and he insisted he was now alright and proved it by being violently sick. Later with a hot cup of tea inside him I saw him stagger off, over Chalkwell Bridge, while I got on my motor bike, still soaking wet, home to a change of clothes and a late dinner, leaving the dinghy full of sand, seaweed and water to be attended to when I returned in the afternoon.

I walked back later along the cinder path, but later going home to tea decided to go over the bridge and up Woodfield Road. At that time, where there are now houses, there was a large field covered with low bushes and hawthorn trees and there, under one of these lay Osker. He had got no further than a few yards from the top of the bridge and was sleeping peacefully, still in his wet clothes. I didn't know whether to disturb him, but decided that he probably dare not go home anyhow, and left him, frightened to think of the things that could happen to him, and equally angry with him at his behaviour.

Next day he turned up, apparently none the worse, again very sorry and full of remorse. But I now knew it was a waste of time to lecture him and we still remained good friends. It did have one advantage. I think he finally realized that he was not welcome, or was ashamed to come again on the beach in the state he had been in. On the few occasions afterwards when he did have too much to drink he would endeavour to pass unnoticed and sleep it off in the corner seat of the shelter under Chalkwell Bridge as, I think, he dared not go home. But these occasions became less frequent as time went on, particularly since he had now become the close friend of Mr. Tye, of "Old Hoppy" I have mentioned elsewhere (in *Joscelyne's Beach*). The two together made an oddly assorted pair, one tall and thin, the other short and stout, and it wasn't long before they were nicknamed "Mutt and Jeff" after two famous cartoon characters in one of the larger daily papers, and it fitted them perfectly.

But it did more. Mr. Tye protected him, both from Osker's so-called "friends" and himself, and there was a remarkable improvement in his behaviour, except those times when "Hoppy" was occupied in getting a living with his rowing boat. But all in all it helped very considerably. Mr. Ostermayer treated his old pal generously and Mr. Tye in turn looked after him and incidentally took over the ferrying I had previously done, so I saw perhaps less of him as time went on. It was a good combination and benefited us all.

"Andy" Salter has no part in this story, other than he was a customer, a character and a likable man, and the first link that leads to my other adventure with Mr. Ostermayer, but I would like to put him in the picture. Tough looking, short and sturdy, looking less

like a yachtsman than anyone I knew, he went sailing in his beautifully built fourteen footer, another product of Gravesend. Always
dressed in his normal working clothes, he made no pretence at
even adopting a yachting hat, or a nautical look, as was general
among those who owned and sailed boots. His love of his boat
was only perhaps exceeded by his love of the fair sex, but that is
entirely another story, but I shan't tell it. But for all that, he was a
"man's man" and he was on the beach only a very little while
before he was surrounded by a group of laughing and chattering
males. He had unlimited stories, mostly "risqué", many jokes and
a general good humour that made him quite a popular figure, and
I was whenever possible, among his audience. Mother did not
approve of him but was so fond of his old father that she suffered
him.

Most of his conversation and sentences contained an unpleasant four-letter and other swear words, and on first hearing him talk
one was shocked, but it flowed into his conversation so naturally
that it seemed to lose all offensiveness and become just part of his
speech. But equally strange, when in conversation with Mother or
when ladies were present, never once did these words slip into his
speech, nor did he say anything the slightest bit improper.

But it was "old" Mr. Salter, the next link in the chain, whom
both Mother and I were so pleased to see. He visited his son a few
times a year, and invariably came to see us, and when he did it was
the "upholstered" beer crate and a cup of tea by "the shed" door
granted to the select few. He was the dearest old man imaginable,
kind, gentle and interesting. No one would have suspected he had
served his life in sailing ships, among perhaps some of the rough-
est and toughest of the flotsam and jetsam that sailed the seven
seas. His quiet and gentle voice, his weathered, brown, contented
face, his blue eyes and white thatch of hair, made him an unre-
peatable character not to be found in this day and age. Although
over seventy he was still working. His job and home at Gravesend
was on a large sailing ship "hulk" converted to a hospital. From its
stumpy mast flew the yellow flag of quarantine and on board he
served the rota of doctors that attended those detained from the
various many ships of all nationalities on their way to the docks of
Tilbury and London. Apart from its natural unpleasantness it was
not a hard job. He was greatly appreciated by those he served and

had comfortable quarters and plenty of spare time, much of which he used to supplement his small wage by making marvellous bow and side rope fend-offs for yachts. It was he that taught me how to make a "Turk's head" and wall and crown and other fancy knots, join a rope in a "long splice" – so joined rope could pass through a pulley – rings that were used for deck tennis and other games on ocean going liners and many other things, fast dying out.

And I regret now that I did not value this knowledge as I should have done, but in those days my life was filled with other things and they, or at least some, are forgotten. Maybe if he had been at hand more often to keep me on my toes it would have been different, but his visits were all too short and far apart for me to learn all he could have taught me, even if I had been willing, which I sometimes now doubt.

The last time he visited us he delighted me by offering me a canoe. It had been picked up in the river, dumped aboard "the hulk" and left there. Now the authorities wanted it disposed of. I could have it if I could remove it, and this is where we again rejoin our story of my adventures with our old friend Mr. Ostermayer.

The offer of the canoe was too good to miss, but how to get it. I toyed with the idea of going by train to Gravesend and pad-dling it down river, but I still had to get to it, in the middle of the tideway. I wondered, should I or could I swim out, only to cross these ideas off as impracticable. But I was determined to have it somehow, and as I thought of one idea after another, who should arrive but Osker. I mentioned my problem, as a matter of interest, and to my surprise without hesitation he said:

"I'll take you up there in my boat."

I accepted his offer with pleasure tempered with some reluc-tance. Would his old "Evinrude" do the journey? Besides, I didn't know the river much higher than Hole Haven, and as far as I knew he had never been much further than All Hallows opposite, but he was sure he could do it and I just hoped he could, or at least his motor could. It was over 35 miles there and back. It had never run so long in its life and was temperamental at the best of times, and I had a suspicion it was nearly worn out already.

He was far more confident than I, but I wanted that canoe badly and throwing caution to the winds, we made plans for the journey. First the tides had to be right. We decided to start at low water as early as possible to catch the five or so hours of the flood, which should bring us to Gravesend at approximately high water and, all being well, come the whole way home on the ebb. By so doing we have the help of the tide both ways and the least strain on the engine. We hoped that nothing unforeseen would happen.

On the day planned it was a quiet cloudy morning with a little sun low on the horizon as I walked down the Crowstone hardway at seven o'clock. There was little or no water in the creek and I made my way over the sandbank to the "Ray", where Osker was waiting with his boat. He had been out all night, having caught the last of the tide the night before, but tucked in his army greatcoat he showed little signs of it. A quick hot cup of tea from my flask, a thick cheese sandwich and we were under way, through the Low Way and out into the river, which was even now helping us on our way.

Canvey and the Chapman lighthouse, Kynocks, Hole Haven, and then unknown inlets and marsh land, gulls and seabirds, odd strange buildings, barges crisscrossing, ships, tugs, coal hulks: it was to me an adventure of a lifetime, and through it all, the engine kept up its steady purr until on the fast, ever-rising tide a mass of ships, houses and all that goes to make up a busy seafaring community told us we had reached Gravesend.

It took little time to find the quarantine hulk, its yellow flag proclaiming to all and sundry its purpose in life. Coming alongside, Mr. Salter, whom I had previously notified, was waiting and close by on the deck was the "canoe", and while I hoped I didn't show it I was extremely disappointed. It was not a bit like the slim, fast Indian or esquimaux canoe I had built up in my imagination. This was a canvas box with pointed and sloping ends built on a framework of galvanized steel tubing about twelve feet long, three feet wide and one foot deep. It looked rather like the work of a semi-skilled amateur but of no particular merit, but would, I thought, provide great fun for the children on our beach, so our trip was not entirely wasted, or so I thought then.

Everything having gone to plan, and just on high water we stopped for a "bite to eat" and coffee already laid on by our host, filled the tank of the outboard and loaded on the canoe. It was difficult and clumsy to stow: upside down it filled most of our boat and even with some three feet protruding over the bows gave us little room, other than a small space in the stern, to work and steer the boat and engine, but it was the best we could do and we turned for home.

The journey up had been kind to us, the river quiet and smooth, but now in the west dark clouds were forming and already several heavy gusts of wind from the same direction were making quite an unpleasant swell and I remember thinking, "Good, this will help us home."

The engine still running sweetly and the wind behind us, we were making rapid progress, but as the river grew wider so the sea grew ever increasingly rougher and the short, steep waves were beginning to splash inboard. And more frightening, added to the sea and wind, a huge black cloud was rapidly forming and over-taking us. A few drops of rain in the wind were the herald of a downpour like a white curtain rapidly coming down river, blotting out everything behind it. I knew it would be only a matter of moments before reaching us, soaking the mass of wiring on the back seat and stopping the engine, so we switched it off and with a struggle pulled the upturned canoe over it and hid ourselves under it for shelter.

It is hard to describe what happened next. At the mercy of a relentless sea and wind, without steerage way, the boat was career-ing out of control, sometimes beam on, sometimes spinning around, a plaything of the elements, all the time shipping water as the boat pitched and rolled while the rain beat down in fury trying to get at us.

And get me it did as I crawled forward in desperation, undid the anchor from the cable and paid out the fifteen fathoms of thick bass cable. This acted as a sea anchor, and slowly but surely it began to ride head on to the waves and wind. But we were still being carried downstream like a bit of driftwood in a millrace.

There was water now well over the floorboard; we were soaked to the skin. The boat, now in mid-stream, was right in the "fair-way" and shipping lane, and looming in the not far distance but rapidly gaining on us was a big cargo ship apparently coming straight towards us. Hauling our anchor rope in I tried to get out the oars, but with the canoe occupying most of the boat it was quite impossible to use them and we were now, once again, out of control, and water up to our ankles, sloshing around.

I thought for sure they will see us and alter course, but its bow was now bearing directly on us, its masts were directly in line, a sure indication that it would pass neither to left nor right of us; it was only a matter of minutes before it crushed us. I was terrified, while for'ard, Mr. Ostermayer was waving and shouting his head off, to no avail.

There was only one way out. With the strength of fear and a mighty heave, I tumbled the canoe overboard. I was now able to use the oars. I yelled at Osker:

"Shut up and get hold of one of these bl***y oars!" I rarely if ever swear, maybe that was the reason it had the desired effect, but it seemed the only alternative to bring his mind back to reality.

With us both straining at the oars, we pulled some six feet from the oncoming bow. The canoe, half submerged a few feet away, disappeared as it caught the full force of the ship's bow, but the bow wave only caught and bounced us sideways, away from the ship and then dumped us back to the rusty iron plates on its water-line. I remember looking up at the great towering wall of steel beside and above us.

Tugging at the oars we pulled away a little, only to be dragged back by the suction of the size and speed of the hull as it rushed through the water. I could now hear and see the tip of a giant pro-peller thrashing the water into a boiling froth, and realized the dan-ger of being drawn into the vortex it created. This drove us to more frantic efforts with the oars, either pushing madly on the ship's side, or attempting to row when we could. It seemed an age, but I suppose it could only have been minutes when drifting and struggling past the revolving blades we found ourselves pitching and tossing in its white foaming wake, rather to my surprise alive and still afloat.

During the whole of this traumatic experience we neither saw nor heard a sign of human life on the vessel. No one, as far as I know, saw us or knew we were there, and as the stern and after-deck became visible on passing, not a movement gave any indica-tion that there was a single person on board. We could have both been drowned and no one the wiser.

I have since heard of similar cases happening in the Estuary and in one case a local amateur angler, fishing opposite Westcliff in the fairway, was run down and by mere chance sighted from

Southend pier clinging onto the ship's rudder, the tips of its huge propeller revolving only a foot or two in front of him. He was six miles below the pier before being rescued.

But back to our story. Still in the shipping lane, still at the mercy of wind, tide and heavy seas, the floorboards awash, the boat was becoming sluggish and unmanageable and we were still in the fairway. In the distance a line of shipping leaving the docks and making towards us made me realize that although the immediate danger was past we were by no means out of trouble, but on the credit side we could now use our oars and the rain had stopped and the sky was clearing, with a promise of sunshine.

So first and foremost our object was to get clear of the shipping. We rowed hard and solidly, but with difficulty, through the amount of water we had shipped, but by taking a diagonal course towards the distant Essex marshes, in spite of everything we were still, with the help of the wind and tide, making good progress home.

Once we were clear of the shipping we baled what water we could out, with a noticeable improvement, and with a brightening sky and the wind we were all drying out a bit. But even so it was still very rough and uncomfortable. The engine was very wet. I continued to row to control our direction and Osker started on his engine. From under the back seat he produced a large tin containing an odd assortment of spanners wrapped up in a large piece of rag, and to my surprise quite dry. With this he was able to dry off most of his equipment, removing and cleaning the sparking plug and various other bits. Eventually after a few coughs and splutters I watched with unbelieving eyes as it started and continued to run, and run it did the whole way home.

We slipped across the tail end of the Ray Sands to escape the tide run of the Low Way, but never made it to the mooring. We anchored off the Crowstone to bring in next day. Tired, wet and hungry, but with a strange, exhilarated feeling that we had fought and beaten the elements, we walked across the mud to "the shed", made tea and home to bed.

It wasn't until I was just dozing off that the thought came. Supposing, just supposing I had done what I had contemplated, gone by train and tried to paddle that unlucky canoe home myself. Would I still be here, tucked up in bed?

For a very long time, except for a few uneventful lapses, Osker went about his daily life. He and Mr. Tye were still close friends: it seemed they needed each other. His marital life continued much the same, except perhaps the roles had changed a little and he was more "the lodger", but he never took me or any other into his confidence, but seemed content.

And it occurs to me now, how very little I did know of my customers' and clients' private lives, and I think the fault, if such it was, could be laid at my doorstep, as I just wasn't interested and encouraged no confidences. My world was "the Beach", what they did on it was my business; their life away from it didn't enter into it and was a thing apart. For this reason I must have missed a great deal of the background of their normal lives and problems.

This happy state of affairs continued; we were still the best of friends and "Old Hoppy" still continued to ferry him back and forth if necessary, but a job I willingly performed should the occasion arise. Our trip to Gravesend was now a thing of the past; he was behaving himself, and had been for some time.

It was late evening on a quiet, warm summer's day, the sea a flat calm, dusk just creeping in, when Mr. Tye, having had a "good day" – meaning he had taken several shillings – landed on the beach. I gave him a hand to pull his boat up above the tide line, ready for next day, and as he limped past the shed door, with a "Good night, Ma'am" to Mother, he turned to me and said:

"Ain't that Osker a funny bloke? He asked me to put him ashore in half an hour, but he ain't there. Did you bring him in?" And he added, "He'd a tidy drop to drink when I put him aboard."

I assured him I had not seen him or brought him ashore, and as far as I knew, neither had anyone else.

I don't know what decided me to bother further; I was meeting a girl friend as soon as Mother went home, and that would be soon. The dusk was deepening, but I could still see there was no one aboard his boat. But there did seem a darker shadow in the water by the bow. I got out my old binoculars, not much to look at but very good even at night (my old friend Captain Woods had brought them from Germany just after the 1914-18 War).

I ran to the end of the beach which was nearest to his boat and with their aid could see something or someone in the water, close to the bow. I shouted to Mr. Tye:

"I believe he's overboard." With all haste we relaunched his boat and I rowed all out to reach Osker's boat moored some seventy yards off shore, only this time he was the mooring link. With his right hand holding his mooring buoy and his left holding the gunwale at the bow end of his boat, he joined the two together.

The buoy to some degree was keeping him afloat and, being high tide and completely calm, he had been able to support himself, since he had been pulled or fallen overboard in picking up his moorings. Fortunately he had stopped the motor before, otherwise the boat would have careered off, leaving no other support than the buoy, and leaving him in danger of drowning, as he never could swim.

But even as it was, it would only be a matter of time before the ebb tide, setting in with gathering force, would have dragged the boat from his grasp, leaving him dependent entirely on the small mooring buoy in his other hand.

It was now quite dark, but between us we dragged and heaved him aboard and secured the boat. He was completely drunk and almost unaware of the situation and far beyond the stage when he could have helped himself. If he had shouted, which I doubt, no one had or would have been likely to hear him among the general noises ashore and only a chance remark, I think, saved him from drowning.

Between us we got him ashore and somehow over the bridge. Mr. Tye said he would try to get him home, but he told me next day that Osker had refused to go on, and crawled under his favourite bush still soaking wet. By all the rules he should have died of pneumonia or exposure, or been twisted by rheumatism long ago, but next day, contrite but in the best of health, he turned up with a "peace offering" of a pair of thick woollen sea-boot stockings, which he insisted I had. Neither could I bring myself to be angry with him or tell him off as I intended, and things returned to normal.

. . . Apart from one other instance, when he again lapsed and was unable to control his boat. At full speed it took charge of him and started rushing around in circles among all the moored craft off the foreshore while he stood in the bows waving and shouting, attempting to ward off hitting one moored yacht after another in its mad careering. This lasted half an hour, to a delighted audience on the cinder path, until for some reason it headed straight for "the rocks", as we called the apron wall. It sent him staggering backwards, and he was badly bruised, but it sobered him up considerably. I promised to look after his boat and sent him staggering off, to sleep in his corner seat under the bridge.

These episodes occurred over a large number of years, in fact over most of the time I was on the beach. He was not a confirmed drunkard; most of the time he went about his daily routine neither interfering with, nor bothering, anyone. Much of his failing was encouraged by his "friends" in Old Leigh, some perhaps by his peculiar home life. Maybe his parents ensuring his future without real work were factors all contributing towards these occasional lapses, which became less frequent as time went on.

My association with him led to my brother-in-law, then a lad at school but even then a keen angler, becoming close friends with him and a companion on his fishing trips during holidays and weekends.

Strangely enough he still found sufficient army surplus to maintain his chosen style of dress. He did have a new peaked cap, his old one going back from whence it came, overboard in our ill-fated venture from Gravesend, and a brand new "Evinrude" rested on the stern of his boat, the cause, to some degree of the last episode, owing to its extra power. Mother still had her supply of fish, and through my young brother-in-law I was, in penalty of never being spoken to again, let into Osker's secret method. Even now I wonder if my vow still holds and hope to be forgiven.

It seems that all the crabs he caught were crushed, all his fish cleanings and some strong essence were put in a small sack, weighted and lowered overboard just on the bottom. The tide carrying the flavour of its contents attracted the fish from a considerable distance. It seemed such a simple explanation and method. I was amazed to think that even my Dad didn't know it, and I had always thought he knew all there was about fishing, and if the size of Osker's catches was any indication, it worked.

He never appeared to grow a day older, and I met him frequently after I left the Beach, until the Second World War. When it was over and I returned, he was no longer around; a pity when I could have replenished his wardrobe with my own home guard army overcoat and battledress.

No one seemed to know what had happened to him for sure, but I was told by someone (and I still can't remember who) that he, his wife and lodger had gone in the general evacuation of the town in 1940. My informant added that he had heard that later during the War, Mrs. Ostermayer had died, the "lodger" had found other accommodation and Mr. Ostermayer was living in Brighton with his brother – a relative I never knew existed – and that he had completely given up his drinking habits and was wearing suits and other normal clothing.

But how much of this was fact or only hearsay, I have no real knowledge. In my mind his khaki clad, long, thin, shambling figure still haunts the foreshore of Chalkwell, and I shall never picture him otherwise, and in spite of his failings like him that way best.

13

"Manure"
by any other name

I have often wondered and remarked on that strange twist of fate "chance" or "destiny" that selects for some unknown reason, and completely at random, one of us lesser mortals, for fortune or success, for no particular reason or virtues – other than being in the right place at the right time. I am fully aware that no two of us are likely to react in the same way faced with similar conditions.

So when recently I heard the following little story it brought to mind just such a case that happened locally, told by a member of the local Allotment Society. It seems that at their usual meeting a very knowledgeable and highly successful grower of vegetables, albeit as earthy as those he grew, was due to give a talk to those lesser skilled in the art of husbandry and who failed to produce those large and succulent roots he was famed for.

A committee member with more sensitive feelings was increasingly worried that the speaker's frequent mention of the benefits of "manure" might embarrass the more refined two important members of the mixed audience. So, seeking out the lecturer's wife, he tactfully suggested she should persuade her husband to replace "manure" by fertiliser. To which she replied that she doubted it would do any good, as previously she had had the greatest difficulty in even getting him to call it "manure".

So it prompts me to warn those of a similar sensitive nature that this story is not for them, and having made sure that few will heed my advice (for that very reason) I will continue. It starts in my younger schooldays but has no particular bearing on the facts and it probably wouldn't matter if it were never told and rightly so. But be that as it may, I shall make it part of my narrative.

With the larger families and closer knit communities of those days and lack of traffic on the roads (although we had unlimited fields to play in), the streets were also our playgrounds and the youngsters of the day formed themselves into not so much "gangs" as "tribes". Of these, our own particular "tribe" comprised the Cranleigh Drive and Elm Road children and we were in constant enmity with those of the Leigh Hall Road area. The clearly defined territory of each was divided by a small but deep brook running east and west along the lower section of Elm Road, through a field, south but parallel with what is now Queens Avenue and thence to the London Road. It continued behind Kathleen Drive to discharge into Prittle Brook, but is now completely built over and lost.

The "Leigh Hall tribe" were led by one, who from his father's rather more superior position, clothed him in "knicker bocker" trousers and who was immediately seized on by us and nicknamed "Baggy Trousers". Those who followed him were "The Baggy Trousers Lot". At times we called a truce and considerable trafficking took place with birds eggs and cigarette cards etc. At other times hostility broke out afresh between us and much shouting, threats and missiles crossed the territorial waters that separated us, but rarely ended in anything of serious consequence. This was the period when I first met Bob and his younger brother.

Second in rank to Baggy Trousers (who incidentally later became a much respected and prosperous Estate Agent and Auctioneer), Bob and I were enemies. They lived in Leigh Hall Road, their father a prosperous business man, their lifestyle moved in higher social circles. Later this did not prevent us becoming good friends and old enmities were buried (although what drew us together is long forgotten). But time and circumstance caused our friendship to lapse, brought together only for a moment at the funeral of their sister Barbara, a vivacious and beautiful girl who died in a local motor cycle accident, that brought sorrow and grief to all the family. Later they moved and I saw no more of them.

The Second World War came and went, my memory of our friendship faded and was almost lost. But only now do my opening remarks become apparent or make sense. It was a year or so after the War and my return to Leigh. The buying of "The Orchard" (my new home in the Undercliff Gardens) necessitated a visit to my solicitors in London Road, and as I approached their portals, there, descending the steps from the door, was my old friend, Bob. Not the Bob I knew of yesteryear. This was a new version, expensive and elegantly dressed. A large cigar whose smell alone seemed infinitely superior, and smoke bluer than any I had ever known, puffed contentedly in his full round face. Wealth and prosperity radiated from his very comfortable figure. He had come a long way from the boy I used to know.

We recognized each other immediately as we thrust our hands forward in genuine pleasure in meeting, and our handshake was, for all the long years apart, full of warmth.

I looked at him with both surprise and admiration and blurted out "Holy Smoke" Bob. (Perhaps it was the cigar that prompted it.) You look like "a million dollars", so blooming prosperous. Perhaps not the best chosen introduction, after so many years, but it was obvious the praise pleased him.

His next words had the same effect on me as a sudden blow between the eyes: "So I ought. I'm up to my neck in sh*t."

Speechless, stunned and bewildered, I looked at him, to see if he was joking. I saw no sign of it. It was in any case a strange way of renewing an old friendship, but for all that, the immediate impact on me seemed to delight him.

He smiled at the effect his words produced. I have since felt that maybe I wasn't the first to be greeted so. Yes he said, and once again repeated his previous statement, as a follow up blow to make fully sure I had heard a-right.

Having fully enjoyed the devastating blow he had so suddenly and unexpectedly assailed me with, he then changed the subject, asked after the family, and tried to pack a lifetime's news since last we met into a few minutes. Then, he replaced and puffed his cigar, consulted a large gold wrist watch, put out his hand and said, "well must be off now, time's money, jolly nice seein' you again," and made to walk off.

I stood in his path. "Oh no you don't Bob. If you can't afford to lend me ten minutes of that precious so and so time, after all these years of knowing each other, things have come to a pretty bad state for both of us. We meet after thirty odd years, you bewitch and bewilder me with a wild and ridiculous statement and then "push off" without a word of explanation. Come off it Bob. Cut your story to its bare limits if you like but let me at least hear what it's all about and what sh*t has got to do with it because it certainly doesn't seem to have done you any harm.

He hesitated, weighing up the time lost against the pride of achievement. "O.K." he replied, let's sit in the car, and he led me across the road to a large and highly polished limousine. Seated in deep upholstered comfort, this was his story.

And it proves, not only large vegetables, but also large businesses can grow on this much despised product, irrespective of what it may be called. After his parents' death, he and his brother had moved out to the Dawes Heath Road, then deep in the countryside, and started a business with reasonable success, making small portable sheds and wooden buildings. They had no sewerage system in the area. Like those around them, they were served by a cess-pit, and as these need pumping out at frequent intervals, the brothers invested in a pump and did the job themselves, and later developed it as a sideline among their neighbours and a great convenience to those around them. It later led to them having cards printed, advertising their service and assuming the title of "Sanitary Engineers". This thereby unknowingly altered the course of their future lives, although at the time it merely supplemented their income. This was the situation at the outbreak of the Second World War.

What caused them to both volunteer and join the Air Force he failed to mention, but he did mention they were allowed to remain together. The first six months was a period of boring inactivity as they were only engaged on ordinary ground staff duties here in England.

So when suddenly their Commanding Officer called Bob to his office and informed him that he had received a letter from the Borough Surveyor of Southend on Sea, Essex, asking his permission for Bob to be granted leave to visit him on important Government business, it made not only an unanswerable mystery at this strange request, but a very welcome break from the monotony of service life. Something they both were beginning to regret.

With three days' leave he caught the train to Southend, now a ghost town with most of its inhabitants dispersed and evacuated and, still wondering what on earth it was all about, presented himself to the Borough Surveyor, only to be met by a blank face and no knowledge of the need for his presence or the reason for his summons, until someone tentatively suggested he contacted the Sanitary Engineers Department instead.

87

And here he was welcomed, "Ha, Mr. P****, I see you are a Sanitary Engineer." The man consulted a card that lay on his desk, and which by some strange chance had come into his possession (one of the few printed). Without querying Bob's experience or capabilities, he started to unravel the puzzle of the whole mysterious business that had brought him there. Then the official continued: "Would you be prepared to consider the contract for the removal of the contents of the toilet buckets from Shoebury Garrison."

Taken completely by surprise, Bob explained his commitment to the R.A.F., only to be informed that could be taken care of without difficulty. He was then told the job involved the removal of some two hundred buckets at one shilling (old money) per bucket. Making a quick calculation his mind registered a sum of £10, and £10 week was a very considerable amount in those far off days. But even more attractive, it offered an escape from the dull uneventful life that they were having at that particular time in the services. He suggested that it would be necessary that his brother be allowed to assist him and was assured that this also could be "arranged". This was amicably agreed, details gone into, and the wheels set in motion. But just as Bob was about to leave, he was staggered by his interviewer's last words:

"By the way Mr. P****, you of course realize it is two hundred buckets *a day* – seven days a week."

Their release came through with unexpected and commendable speed, the pump renovated, an old water tank mounted on an equally ancient lorry, and they were in business.

And it is here that I openly admit that given this same opportunity my character would have reacted totally differently. I would have probably refused such an unpleasant means of living and not recognized its possibilities as Bob did.

Evidently, their service proved highly satisfactory, as shortly afterwards they were offered and accepted the contract for the whole of Eastern Command, and later the even larger Southern Command which constituted the lower half of England. And from then on they never looked back.

At the time of our meeting they had seventy huge tankers in service and a "spin off" market for the contents to be processed into "fertiliser", and also a firm foothold in the ever increasing industrial waste disposal trade with even more profitable prospects.

Their tankers are still on the roads, their shares high on the stock market. But Bob is no longer with us to enjoy the fruits of his success. When I left him that day, it was the last I saw of him. He moved in different circles and our paths didn't cross again, and how much his wealth contributed to his early departure I can only guess. I have purposely not mentioned his name. Those of my generation who lived hereabouts may well remember him; to those that just read his story it won't matter. But look out for those big tankers as they pass. In big letters it still exists.

14

The Story of the "Robin Redbreast"

My knowledge of spiritualism is very little, almost a closed book, but equally I keep an open mind. Frankly I don't know. It would seem the only way to prove its reality is to die and, as I hope to leave that as long as possible, it will remain unproven to me.

It was, in my youth, almost an improper subject. While the Clergy and Church were busy describing the delights of the here-after in Heaven, they showed a singular objection to the inhabitants of this planet sending or receiving any message of hope or confirmation from those in the promised land. There was a brief respite when such eminent people as Sir Arthur Conan Doyle, the well-known author, and Sir Oliver Lodge, the highly respected scientist, became staunch upholders of the spiritualistic faith, but largely due to the ease in which it lent itself to rogues and charlatans, it then faded out of the public eye. Recently U.F.O.s, equally controversial, have taken its place.

My first actual encounter with a spiritualist was in my early days on the Beach, around 1920. Mr. Lambert was tall, thin, his clothes hung on him like a sack. His moustached and bearded face and gaunt thin cheeks were forgotten when one looked into his eyes, gentle, kindly and warm. They reflected his nature and no man would have made a better or more suitable model of our Saviour in the hands of either sculptor or artist. A bachelor, he worked (I think) in the Ministry of Fisheries as a research chemist and I made his acquaintance in a somewhat unusual manner. It was my custom to take a small trawl I had made to two large ponds (now much smaller) just by the Crowstone, when the tide receded, and for fun, trawl for eels or anything that swam, left behind by the tide in them.

One evening I caught an eel-pouting, a fish I think uneatable, and now rarely ever seen (or perhaps that was not its real name but just a local one) and someone suggested that I should take it to Mr. Lambert.

He was delighted and even more so when, put in a pail of water, it gave birth to some sixty of seventy baby fish (which were put in the water at London Bridge the following morning.) From then on he would visit me, mostly accompanied by his aged, blind father who depended on him for almost everything, and who he looked after, with the devotion and care of both nurse and loving daughter rather than son.

When his father died he was heart-broken. He turned to spiritualism to try and contact him by joining a nearby spiritualism church, and on his occasional visits told me that he was receiving messages through a contact in this church. How much faith I had in this is difficult to assess. At the time I wasn't particularly interested (as I might be now) but it gave him great comfort and that in itself was sufficient reason not to attempt to council him otherwise.

But it was later when he told me a curious story of a model boat he had bought on holiday in Hastings, a beautiful model of a large sailing vessel called the "Robin Redbreast". Its previous owner knew nothing of its history and cared less, which if anything increased its new owner's desire to find out more about it. But try as he would, by visiting maritime museums and libraries etc., he could find no knowledge of the real ship that he was sure was its inspiration and he had almost given up hope of ever learning its true story. But he grew to love and cherish it. A lonely man, no one to care for, with the death of his beloved parent he slowly gave up the outside world and lived within himself. Just occasionally he came to see me for a chat, mostly about the mystery of the "Robin Redbreast", or perhaps a message from his father, usually so casual and lacking detail as to be little proof in my mind of its authenticity.

Then one day, after some hesitation as to my reaction, he startled me with the claim that occasionally, when in bed, his spirit left his body and hovered over it, and he found himself looking down on his earthly body lying there, and it took considerable will-power on his part to return to it. He seemed in no way perturbed or upset by this, in fact quite the reverse. It was a joyful experience which he said left him with little or no fear of dying.

I was horrified at these disclosures, thinking it was early signs of a mental illness but in all other respects he seemed perfectly sane and normal. I have since learned that this is an experience particularly felt by those facing a crisis, in a serious illness, and was in fact personally experienced by one who is nearest and dearest to me and in whom I have infinite faith of the truth of this uncanny happening.

But at that time I was unaware of such things and extremely worried that his mind was going. I was greatly relieved when a subtle change came over him. He seemed anxious to pick up the threads of life again when a new medium on a visit to his church delighted him by contacting and claiming that she was in touch with his father.

Certainly it was very mystifying. The message contained details and information of much that was personal between them, intimate happenings that it was doubtful or even impossible for others to know of. It completely convinced him he was now in direct communication with his deceased father and the little he told me almost convinced me also, but true or false it had a marked and very noticeable effect on him for the better.

The medium's visits were the highlights of his uneventful existence, and culminated on one Sunday when she announced a message from "the beyond" which he was sure (although no names were mentioned) was for him. The wording was that of his father, and had the ring of a genuine communication that left no doubts in his mind, so he told me later. With the usual customary declarations, the voice directed that the listener should walk slowly and observe that which was around him through a well known street in London, where that which had troubled him so long would be answered.

So sure was Mr. Lambert that the message was for him that a few days later he put words into action and went to London, to the street mentioned. It was a street composed almost entirely of bookshops, art, and bric-a-brac and, as he slowly sauntered past one of the smaller shops, hanging on a wall just above the clutter of old books and other oddments was the painting of a fine ship.

It had such a familiar look that it hardly surprised him to see its name. He knew it instinctively, but there it was for all to see, the "Robin Redbreast" and beneath this, all the details of its builders, tonnage, age and ports of call, in fact almost everything of her early history he had so long desired to know.

If the shop keeper had asked a fortune for it I think somehow he would have still bought it, but it was reasonably priced and purchased immediately, as Mr. Lambert explained his interest and long quest. But having doubts of the shopkeeper's ability to understand what had led him there, he discreetly abstained from volunteering further information. With his find safely packed, and a pleasant conversation, he was about to leave when the shopkeeper said, "Just one moment sir. I think I have something else that might interest you, it came with the picture." Rummaging along a shelf packed with books, searching for some time, he selected one and handed it over for inspection.

Mr. Lambert was amazed to read the title, "The voyages of the Robin Redbreast," by Capt. Earnshaw. He just could not believe his eyes. Here for sure was the answer to all the questions that had so long avoided him. His happiness was complete. From then on he came once more alive and life once again was worth living.

The picture took pride of place in his living room, the book beneath on his desk. The model prominently displayed was all he asked of life, with many questions answered. But now, with added interest, he contacted the publishers, hoping to contact relatives of the author, and this he did. They informed him that the author himself at the age of 90 had only died very recently, naming the date of his decease, and a picture of his gravestone. Strangely enough it was the day before Mr. Lambert had received his message. He died several years later. Perhaps he found the answers to much that still puzzles me.

The model, book and picture reside in a maritime museum in London, but few of those that view them know or would believe in the story they hide.

15

A Family Affair

It was long after I had ceased to wonder where truth began and fiction ended, with the story of the "Robin Redbreast". Mr. Lambert was no longer with us and much was unexplained, with no hope of answers, so I left it at that. I then had my next contact with spiritualism, although if truth were known the only part it played was that the lady involved claimed she was a medium and in touch with those who had passed on. But to my mind, it was more "second sight", "fortune telling", or just plain chicanery, but which of these I am still to find an answer, and I leave it to those who read this to form their own judgement.

This time it was on my own doorstep, in fact inside my immediate family circle, so I can be more accurate with the facts than previously. There is still a great deal I don't know, and I have no wish to probe into the intimate details surrounding this little story, which in fact may hardly be worth recording, other than for those directly interested.

My sister Edna was the only one that took after my father, dark haired, hazel eyes and slightly swarthy complexion. She had grown into a lovely girl, then misfortune in the shape of a serious illness struck her. The treatment at the time was not fully understood, but after undergoing a dangerous operation, she pulled through and was able to resume normal life, but from time to time the illness reappeared, and she underwent further operations, each time getting better for a while. It was during one of these periods of better health she met and married John Barr, the son of a family who were personal friends and frequent visitors to our Beach.

The marriage was a "love match" from the start, they were devoted to each other. It was that story-book love that one reads about. He was a gentle and caring husband and during the times when illness returned, nursed her with a love and devotion that was exceptional. In spite of her poor health, they had a daughter, Jean, to care for also, no easy task, when it was necessary to be at work in London all day.

When the final blow came and my sister died, he was desolated, and although he still had his daughter Jean, his life, like that of Mr. Lambert, seemed empty and without purpose. Unlike him he did not seek solace from spiritualism, although he felt Edna's presence constantly with him and around the house. In these unhappy days, I used to visit him once or twice a week to distract his attention and give him some little help and companionship to ease his loss, and also I greatly admired and was grateful for the care and devotion he had given my sister.

When he arrived home each day, it was necessary to prepare a meal for both Jean and himself, and it didn't surprise me when one evening on my visit, he mentioned that he had made arrangements to continue on to Westcliff and for Jean to go to a boarding house there, run by a Mrs. Owen, to have an evening meal. It was seemingly a sensible plan and worked quite well.

Then he began to change. He spoke more and more of the landlady, a person some thirty years older than himself, and even began to see the likeness of Edna in her. She claimed to be a medium, but even more, she claimed and convinced John that Edna's spirit was close to them, and spoke through her to him. Only little bits of this came out during my visits and I had no real idea of the influence she was slowly but surely exerting on him, until I think she succeeded in convincing John she really was the embodiment of Edna, his lost wife. I had never met her, but on one of my evening visits, the phone rang (after John and Jean had returned from Westcliff, this became a regular practice). It was Mrs. Owen. She said, "Hello John, you've got a visitor with you."

"Yes," my brother-in-law replied (I suppose this was not surprising, since she must have known of my regular visits). A few more words passed and John turned to me. "She says you have had an exciting day." This was true, in fact almost an understatement, but how she knew it was beyond my comprehension.

In the morning, an estate agent had called on us offering my brother and I a piece of land in Sandowne Avenue, Westcliff. Not a proper building plot, but the far end of two gardens. As others were also interested, there was no time to waste. It necessitated planning permission, bank loans, legal aspects, neighbours' objections and a whole host of problems that had sent us rushing around all day, but by evening it was bought and settled, apart from legal niceties. A day to remember, but as we ourselves had known nothing of it before that morning and neither John or anyone he knew could have either, it puzzled me completely.

Intrigued, I said, "Ask her what made us so busy." Back came the reply. "It concerns some land, but not ordinary land, this is surrounded by fences and flowers," which in fact was right. Even more puzzled, I said, "Ask her where it is."

John conveyed the question and she replied, "It's near a large open space surrounded by big trees." As Chalkwell Park (at that time surrounded by huge elms) was only a short distance to the south, I was forced to admit she could be right and, as I couldn't think of anything else at the time to test what seemed her uncanny knowledge, left it at that.

Of course, one could argue it was very inconclusive, just a shot in the dark, any fortune teller at a fair probably could do as good, but John was convinced of her psychic powers and tried equally hard to convince me. Not very successfully, but it certainly left room for explanation.

So I determined to try again, when, some weeks later on my usual visit, the now familiar phone call came through and the usual greeting, "You have a visitor."

About this time, I had an old property I wished to sell, but in spite of "doing it up" it hung fire and I just couldn't find a purchaser and was getting impatient. So during a lull in his conversation, I said, "Ask her when I am going to sell my house in Landsdown Avenue." I still had the doubtful hope I might prove something, one way or another. There was a short silence, then she said, "About the middle of the week, some Jewish people will look at it and buy it." Then she added, "It's a pity about the drains." I turned to John, "What's wrong with the drains? I've looked at them and there's nothing the matter as far as I can see with them." John pointed this out to her, but she still insisted that they needed repair and that was how it was left.

Early next morning, I made a thorough examination of the drainage system and was delighted I had proved her wrong, but had I? Leaving by the back gate into the narrow passage dividing the next pair of houses, I saw their gate was also open. By the side of it was their kitchen gulley and drain, cracked and broken, and a large hole where more water poured through, rather than its correct channel. It was saturating the foundations of both houses and was the direct cause of the dampness that had been a constant source of trouble previously, so once again I was left in doubt.

I quickly obtained permission to do the necessary repairs and awaited the prophesy of midweek. Sure enough, on the Wednesday morning, an agent rang me up, "I am bringing some people to look at your property this afternoon, and would like you to be there."

This time I was sure I had sold it, she had said midweek, and now it happened, and when the prospective clients turned out to be the well known Jewish shopkeepers in Leigh Broadway, "Nina Kays", I was more convinced than ever, not only that I had sold my house, but that I had sorely misjudged Mrs. Owen. But that was the last I saw of them, the sale fell through and again the old doubts returned and remain so to this day.

The next thing I knew was Mrs. Owen had left her boarding house and husband and taken up residence in John's home. She had, foolish as it may seem, hypnotised (the only explanation I can offer) John into thinking she was the incarnation of my sister Edna. She took over completely both John and his home.

I was shocked when I saw her for the first time. I had pictured her as a dark handsome woman, in fact an older replica of my sister, a little like a fortune teller because that is the conclusion I had finally arrived at. But instead she was a grey haired, dirty, untidy woman of doubtful origin and unpleasant manner, accompanied by a huge dog that smothered the whole house in dogs hairs and annexed John's favourite chair by the fireside.

What on earth had possessed him, I cannot even contemplate, nor will I to this day. After a while, I had long given up visiting, although I was still friends with John. He decided to sell his home in Dundonald Drive, and under the influence of Mrs. Owen cut all ties with the family and buy a houseboat to live in on the Medway at Rochester. Even the sale of his house had a peculiar twist to it.

I was decorating a property a few doors away when John had just decided to move. An elderly couple came down the road, stopped and watched me working. Sensing a possible customer, I came down the ladder, and passed the time of day. In a moment we were in conversation and almost immediately they explained they wished to live in or near the vicinity. They were spiritualists and were taking over the small chapel at the top of the road. But the mystery deepened still more when they introduced themselves as Mr. & Mrs. Owen.

I suggested they called on John. They bought his bungalow immediately. John's Mrs. Owen claimed it was all her doing and they claimed to have been guided there. Who was responsible for this strange coincidence, I am not sure, but the part I played in it was never noticed.

It was years after when I saw John again. Mrs. Owen had died, his daughter Jean married and he had also married again, a widow with two young children, the houseboat sold. He was on his last visit to relatives before embarking on a new life in Australia, where he still is. This chapter in his life is, I hope, now completely forgotten. And what of Mrs. Owen? I still haven't found a satisfactory answer.

BE SURE YOUR SINS . . .

It was several months after John had left Leigh and I was chatting with a mutual friend. He asked after John and the conversation came round to the subject of Mrs. Owen, particularly the guesswork or other means of her seemingly strange knowledge.

He dismissed the whole story as humbug. All mediums, in his eyes, were rogues and their church a snare and delusion, and with this sweeping statement summed up his opinion and told me the following little story to prove it. It is I think, maybe, worth recording if only to show poetic justice does sometimes catch up with those that deserve it.

It happened locally, and as my informant was a near neighbour – and it is generally accepted that neighbours know more of the "goings on next door" than the actual participants – I would believe that most of it is accurate. In fact I do have a vague recollection of reading something of it in the *Southend Standard* at the time.

Having no knowledge or personal connection, or ever having met those involved, it left no lasting impression. But I listened to the story with interest.

The person involved was suddenly left a widow by her husband suffering a heart attack and dying. Like both John and Mr. Lambert, she had a very strong attachment and affection for him.

98

They had had a devoted and happy life together, apart, perhaps, a little by her husband's one fault – gambling on horses – which was his sole hobby and interest, when he retired. But she had grown accustomed to it, and accepted it with good will. In fact she was almost willing to encourage it, if it made him happy and kept within bounds.

She was heartbroken and lost, but felt his presence was still near her. If only she could understand how to contact him. With this in mind she assumed she could do so through a medium of the Spiritualistic Church. This she did. In a short while the medium announced she was in touch with the deceased husband, and a message of comfort and assurance of his well-being was received and was welcomed with both belief and joy by the now comforted widow.

This state of affairs continued for some time, the medium was a regular caller – each time with more welcome news of the departed. She soon became a firm friend and associate of the widow, who was not particularly surprised when she received a message through her friend, from her husband imploring her to put all her available cash on a certain horse running in a famous race later that week. So sure was she that the information was correct, she cashed all her savings and placed it all on the horse to win as instructed.

The remarkable part is that the horse did win. Overjoyed, the widow collected her winnings of £1,200, a huge sum for that time, and to show her gratitude wrote a cheque for £400 as a gift for her friend the medium. It was here that her true character showed. Instead of being grateful for the gift she pointed out that, but for her, the widow would have had nothing and it was through her and her contact with the husband she had received such a windfall. She also had had a message from the husband that he wished them both to share it equally.

So completely did the winner have faith that it was her husband's wish, she didn't query or argue, but wrote another cheque for £200, making it £600 she had parted with.

Delighted with sudden wealth, and a message from her husband that she should now visit her surviving relatives in Australia and take full advantage of his gift, the idea appealed to the widow. A passage was booked and a happy six months passed in Australia.

A passage home followed, and it was on that passage misfortune hit her.

A fatal tropical disease, caught at the port of call, overwhelmed her and she died before reaching England. She left no will. The administrators of her estate, going through her affairs found the cashed cheques to the medium among them, and queried the reason. The medium said they were gifts. The lawyers said such large sums could surely not be gifts when the medium had always been paid small sums for her services. Was it not money received under false pretences or under duress? She denied it, in any case she had spent it all and would not and could not return it.

The upshot was she was taken to court and the case went against her. To find the money and costs she was forced to sell her house to pay back to the estate the money she had received. Whether the husband got in touch with her after that I have no means of knowing and neither did the neighbour who was my informant, but as he remarked, "Be sure your sins will find you out." How right he was.

16

The "Old Wreck"

Time, once a friend, but now my enemy, has given me an ultimatum. Tell that story now, neither you nor I can wait. You are the only one left to tell it and soon I shall bury it as deep in the sands of the past as it now lies interred in the "Leigh Middle Sands" and long forgotten.

Seeking an excuse, I said "But is it worth the telling?" He replied, that is not for you or me to decide. The answer will be given by those who read it. But if you need excuses, console yourself that it concerns Old Leigh and that must surely be of interest to those who love its past.

Once again I tried.

"But I only know what my father told me and that was long ago." I could see he was losing patience. Back came the answer: an artist does not necessarily paint everything he sees on his canvas. He paints what he *wants* to see, but keeps within the bounds of truth to convey the reality to those that seek it. Paint your picture in words of your own making. You know the setting, you have seen the river in all its moods, and as a child, the very same craft that sailed it. Write from your heart, you will be forgiven if it is not entirely accurate in every detail, let history judge, that's all I ask.

It was afternoon, but could well have been late evening. An unnatural darkness over-shadowed a dirty, restless sea. Darker shadows foot-printed the heavy squalls of wind and rain that ran wild over it, whipping the wave-tops into a frenzy of white water and foam as they rode roughshod in a mad race to nowhere. Above in the sky, the dark, glowering clouds chased each other in wild abandon, dragging their murky skirts over the distant Langdon Hills in a slurry of grey mist, joining earth and sky as one, spilling their contents on the earth below.

On the Kentish shore, they joined and lost themselves in a background of darkness and swirling cloud, broken for a moment by a patch of light, opening like the shutter of a camera to take a picture and record the struggle going on below it. The schooner (schooners have two masts, rigged fore aft), black and work-stained, slowly fought her way against the fast ebbing tide and wild waters. Overloaded and under-canvassed, it was heavy going. Taut sails, wet and dirty, were "close hauled", both main and mizzen fully reefed and a scrap of canvas for a foresail. Even so, her decks and lee rail were awash, and the wave-tops, like Satan's imps, skipped over the for'ard rail, danced a hornpipe on the fore-deck, played hide and seek in every nook and cranny of the main deck, and then slipped back from whence they came, through the scuppers gurgling with delight at the misery they had left behind.

The skipper, wet, weary, and tired after a sleepless night, struggled with the wheel. Responsibility lay heavily on his shoulders, now of all times he could not afford to make an error. The channel he was seeking left little room for mistakes in this atrocious weather, but once found, offered sufficient water to ride in comfort, protected on the north by the Marsh End Sands, and from the busy sea-going traffic of the main fairway by the Leigh Middle Sands, whose long protecting arm lay just below the surface at low water to the south. He knew it well, had moored there many times previously, but never once in such conditions as this.

The mate and crew waited with unconcealed impatience, they had had more than enough this voyage. The skipper swung the wheel hard over, deep in soaking spray, blocks and cordage rattling, sails lashing the air with a wet mist, and those suffering cries that only a sailing ship can make in heavy weather. The vessel came "head to wind" and slowly lost way.

Orders, almost lost in the elements, rang out: "Lower main and mizzen, take in the foresail, and let go the hook [anchor]."

The tired crew found a hidden strength, they needed no prompting. In surprisingly quick time the sails were furled and the ship was riding to anchor. The darkness was deepening and they had found their haven only just in time.

The skipper left the wheel, his ordeal over. He glanced with approval as black smoke whipped out of the galley stove pipe and lost itself in the wind. A mug of hot strong tea and a bite of something warm to eat, but even more a change into dry clothes, were pleasant thoughts as he stepped down the narrow stairway to the comfort of his tiny cabin, aft. Passing the bulkhead he tapped the barometer fastened there, as was his usual practice, born of long years of habit, paused, and tapped a second time in unbelieving surprise. In all his years at sea, he had never seen it register so low. He offered up a silent prayer. Thank God I'm here and not in the channel tonight. His thoughts were interrupted, the mate lowered a steaming jug of tea down the hatchway. He knew a bite of warm grub would follow.

The wind danced to tunes in the rigging that no instrument made by man could imitate. Masts and spars creaked in accompaniment, the wave tops still played games on her deck as the vessel strained and tugged at her anchor cable. Even now, although she had found her haven, she found no peace. But below decks all was well. Both skipper and crew were grateful their ordeal was finished, at least for the time being.

Tomorrow or maybe next day, when this storm had blown itself out, "Old John" would come in his skiff, pilot them into Leigh on the high water and tie up at Bell Wharf. It was a hard and filthy job, unloading their cargo of "China Clay" for the Victoria Potteries "up the hill". But the boxes of penny clay pipes, destined for London, were different, easily handled and quickly despatched by train. Anyway, it was all in the day's work, and the pubs in Leigh were to a sailorman's liking and comfort, their inmates friendly.

The future grew brighter as they looked to the morrow. It was a hard and unrewarding life, but they knew no other, and wearied by their long voyage from Cornwall, their wet clothes steaming as they hung by the galley stove, they turned in and slept.

The year was 1881, the day, the eve of the "Great Storm". The "Great Storm" like the rest of my story is lost in the past but its consequences were far reaching and left a trail of chaos and suffering throughout southern England, from Cornwall to the North Sea and beyond.

It took its toll in death, torn down stacks and chimneys, gaping holes in roofs, littered streets with broken tiles and slates and flooded homes. And history has it that, in Windsor Great Park alone, over 700 oak trees were uprooted and destroyed. Leigh, like many other villages in its path, paid dearly as the elements ran wild and nature showed the insignificance of man's creation. Those inland suffered, but in no way paid the price it demanded, as did the village that lay beneath the shadow of St. Clements Church.

The gale, with ever increasing force, struck at midnight on the rising tide. Soon their tiny homes lining the single street that ran parallel with the seashore were flooded and knee deep in water. The air was full of flying missiles, as roofs, tiles and chimney stacks caught the full fury of the storm, and legend tells of a heavy barge's dinghy being flung over the railway's six-foot railing fence and forty feet beyond. The inhabitants, mostly fishermen, shivering with cold and apprehension in the doubtful shelter of their bedrooms, wondered at the fate of their boats, their only source of a living, and a desperately hard one at that.

At first light and receding waters, they viewed the havoc of mud, water, and debris that surrounded them and their only street. The damage was disastrous, but by the mercy of providence, some said, or according to others, the shelter of the Leigh Marshes – that formed a natural harbour – most of the larger boats had survived. To compensate again, it was said by some, that same providence provided a sea-shore strewn with valuable wreckage and cargo of ships that had been less fortunate, anchored in the deeper waters of the fairway. Among them was the schooner from Cornwall, whose two masts showing at low water marked her grave. Even they in time disappeared, and her resting place, like so many others, was lost in the murky depths of the river.

No information, as far as I know, exists of the fate of her crew. There is no record of their burial locally, but it is extremely unlikely they survived. Neither boat nor crew belonged to Leigh, maybe that is why its memory faded so quickly. Or was it that in Leigh they had more than sufficient troubles of their own at that time to care.

It was some twenty or more years later, by strange chance my father resurrected its memory, but even so, only for himself and later shared with me. It was our secret, and as such it remained.

He was born in Old Leigh as were many generations before him. Dogged by ill-health in his youth and spoilt by both his widowed mother and in lesser degree by his older spinster sister, (my Auntie Polly), he never knew the discipline of apprenticeship or regular job. And according to my auntie, he suffered severely from asthma, and the possibility of early death. Free of all restrictions, he roamed the seashore, fished, sailed his little boat and lived the life of a beachcomber.

Perhaps he helped out when well enough with odd jobs, and paid his way by his contributions to the family larder of fish and shellfish, or to the fire with driftwood, collected on his wanderings. His passion was fishing, and in time he knew all or most of the more prolific spots where his quarry abounded and rarely returned home in his old "Barges" dingy without a good catch.

But on this one particular day his luck was out. Catching the last of the tide, down Leigh Creek, he waited in the Ray Channel until it uncovered the sand banks, dug sufficient bait for his needs and still had enough ebb to take him to one of his favourite fishing grounds – the "Stone Heap" halfway between the pier head and the Low Way buoy. But never a fish bite came his way. There were crabs in abundance, to eat his precious bait, but that was all. The fish were just not there.

Maybe he would try the "Four Buoys", a rectangle marked by red and white buoys at each corner, that charted and encompassed a strange deep hole, dug by conflicting tides and currents in the sea bed and now a dumping ground for London's rubbish, brought down river by "hoppers" – vessels like ugly overgrown barges, unclean beasts with bottoms that opened and deposited their contents in this convenience so aptly provided by nature, and usually a happy hunting ground for the denizens of the deep.

Dad made his way towards them, a heavy pull, against wind and tide. He was only halfway and still had a mile to go. Best that he threw his anchor overboard and wait the turn of the tide. Not much good putting a line over, and wasting bait. The fish if any, would be around his destination, not here. But maybe a stray . . . He baited his line and dropped it overboard.

It had hardly touched bottom before the sharp tug-tug of a fish responded. He had surely struck a fine fish this time, but it was three, one on each hook. Fine sizeable codling, and so it continued until his line caught fast and he was forced to break it. He soon set up another set of tackle and his success was repeated, but so also was his loss of line, and so it went on, until his weights and hooks were all lost. But what a catch, a day to remember, fine whiting, codling and pouting filled his bag. It was time to go home and in any case he had neither bait nor gear left to fish with.

He went to hoist his anchor. It was caught fast in something, and try as he would, he couldn't lift it. It had fouled that same something that had robbed him of his tackle. He tried again, without success, the chain cable, unlike rope, could not be cut. It must all be lost, but there was an alternative, undo the shackle and let it go in the hope of retrieving it next day, with help. Tying a length of line on the cable end, and an old lifebelt he carried in the back locker on the other, he cast it overboard. But before he left he took careful markings on the shore line to pinpoint the spot. Although he didn't know it then, he had found the "Old Wreck" – the schooner of long ago – or more possibly the "Old Wreck" had found him.

Next day, he took his brother (my Uncle Harry) with him and after considerable searching, found his abandoned anchor and chain. They repeated the previous day's successful fishing and less successful loss of tackle, and proved it was no accident of chance that fish were there in abundance. Dad made all his own weights, and hooks, two shillings and sixpence a box of one hundred, so the loss entailed was very little.

The time came to leave and with the help of the rising tide and their combined efforts they broke the anchor free. They not only brought it to the surface, but with it a large piece of moulded timber, waterlogged, barnacle covered, and riddled with sea-worms. No wonder the fish found it a happy hunting ground. But it did more. It proved it was a wreck and not a mass of old wire cable or rubbish cast overboard by some passing vessel.

It would be a "seven days wonder" if they revealed their find, but an everlasting supply of fish if they kept it to themselves. They agreed it was "finders keepers" so it continued to remain hidden and undisturbed beneath the waters of the Estuary.

When tides and conditions were right, Dad would visit the "Old Wreck", for so he named it, and that was its name from then on. He now knew by careful and discreet inquiry the story of the schooner and its loss, but if Dad knew its name he never told me. The "Old Un's" in The Smack or Ship, with a little prompting and a glass of "Fourpenny", waxed eloquently on the great gale which lost nothing in its telling, and the ill-fated vessel, destined for Leigh with its pipes and china clay was for a brief moment resurrected. Dad still fished in his usual places. Only when the tide and conditions were right did he visit "The Wreck". So it raised no comment or curiosity, at his occasional exceptionally large catches.

Time passed, later still he married and had a family. I was his firstborn, and when I grew old enough was his constant companion. He taught me the ways of the sea – the sand banks and tides of the Estuary. And to my everlasting joy, the hiding place of the "Old Wreck", where his superior skill as a fisherman made little or no difference and I was his equal – a situation that seldom, if ever, occurred elsewhere and to me a great source of satisfaction.

Not only that, he showed me how to find it, and the two pairs of marks that had to be lined up, and the key to its whereabouts. One pair was the Low Way buoy in line with the crane on the gasworks jetty, just below the pier entrance in Southend. Unfortunately, the Low Way buoy moved in a considerable radius, controlled by the state and depth of the tide and prevailing wind, so the wreck's position was always difficult to locate, and quite often necessitated several tries before finding it.

It was no use being *near* it, except for an occasional stray the fish lived *in* the wreck, and that was where they had to be caught, right on top of it.

We knew immediately when we had found it, by the quantity and type of fish we caught, and the loss of tackle. It left no doubts. Often, when the tide swung us away, it had to be located a second or even third time, to find the fish again. I lost count of the numbers of weights, hooks and lines we lost, or the number of anchors Dad had to cut adrift (he had learned his lesson and used rope now). But the sheer excitement of the catch amply compensated for any loss.

And it wasn't only fish we dragged from the murky depths. Large "spider" crabs (now seldom seen) were there in abundance. On other occasions we hooked what Dad called "conker" or "conqueror" crabs, those big crabs they sell cooked in fish shops, but we never got one aboard. They always "let go" the hook when we pulled them to the surface, for they were more intelligent than other crabs.

One memorable day we caught a lobster, but dare not claim the achievement lest our secret became known, but the satisfaction remained and I grew to love our "Old Wreck" more every time we visited it.

Another occasion remains particularly in my memory. We had found it, with less difficulty than usual, and the fish were not so much being caught as committing suicide on our hooks as we hauled them in, three at a time on our three hook "paternosters". I lifted my line, surely this was the heaviest fish I had ever caught in my young life, my short rod bent in an alarming bow as I struggled to both hold it steady and to wind it in.

Dad, seeing my desperation, said, "Here give it to me, let me handle it," but in no way was I going to let it go. This was *my* fish, the biggest in my life, and no one, not even Dad, was going to rob me of the joy and thrill of landing it. What could it be? A big cod, a huge skate, maybe a conger eel. All these thoughts flashed through my mind, as time seemed to stand still. I could see Dad was itching to get his hands on my line. Perhaps after all, I should let his superior skill take over but a curious obstinacy kept the rod in my hand.

But I couldn't wind the reel. In desperation, I dragged the rod inboard, and grabbing the line with both hands, slowly and painfully hauled it up foot by foot, hand over hand until I got my catch to the surface. I was very young at that time, maybe seven or eight years old. No doubt it would have been no trouble at all for Dad. But seeing my struggle, and equally curious to see what caused it, we both peered into the depths, as first one large codling on the top hook broke the surface, followed by an equally large second one, but below that some large, unaccountable shape.

A moment more, and my dreams were shattered. My big fish was nothing more than a barnacle covered, sea-worm riddled, rotting length of timber some three feet long. Probably part of the gunwale, so waterlogged that it was difficult to lift aboard.

The codling had supplied "the kicks" and the timber the weight that was my "Big Fish", but at least I had done it myself. That to some degree lessened the disappointment. And the anticipation was marvellous while it lasted.

Those were happy carefree days. But change and circumstances slowly but surely began to make themselves felt. With increasing good health, but more particularly an increasing family and responsibilities, Dad was forced to give up his way of life and earn a living – at first by working for a builder and decorator in Hadleigh, and later as a builder on his own account, and later still, renting that triangle of sand and seaweed by Chalkwell station (the station was not there at that time). That eventually became known as Joscelyne's Beach, and his main source of income, which considerably limited our opportunities to go fishing and sadly restricted our visits to the "Old Wreck". But maybe it made them even more enjoyable, as they now became a very special treat – a treat that now had added benefits.

Some years previously Dad had joined the S.A.A.S. (Southend Amateur Angling Society), the only local society for anglers at that time. He now started to take a more active part in the competitions (using them, most likely as an excuse to salve his conscience, for taking the time off). He also enrolled me as a member, although I doubt I was more than nine years old. His skill and knowledge of local waters and fishing grounds paid dividends and seldom a competition went by without both of us winning a prize. The prizes, apart from the "cup" and the "shield", were usually "money prizes", part of the entrance fee allotted to first, second and third prize. An article of some sort, to its value, had to be bought by the winner before the money (at the next meeting) was paid over. Should a more expensive item be bought, the difference was made up by the purchaser.

And it was my own prizes that got me a fine sea rod, a winch (or reel) and line, hooks, tackle, and much else. Dad also benefited with sea boots, fishing tackle, and other things, one of which was his pride and joy, a vacuum flask, a remarkable new invention then, from Sweden which kept fluids hot for as long as 24 hours, commonplace now, but at that time greatly valued. He got Mother to make a specially thick woollen cover to wrap it in – whether to protect it or to keep it extra warm, because he just couldn't believe it, I don't know. He treasured it and never ceased to wonder how it worked.

And in all this time the "Old Wreck" was our secret standby in special competitions. It never failed us (providing conditions allowed) and our "luck" was the constant envy of other members who, to give them their due, were at great disadvantage being mostly, if not all, complete amateurs with little experience or knowledge of the best grounds or skill of a lifetime that Dad possessed. It was, I think, looking back, very unfair to them.

For three years running Dad won the silver cup by winning the most competitions each year, and on the third win the cup became his property for good. That third year I also won the "shield", the youngest member ever to do so. I was about twelve and I wonder if it still holds good today.

On several occasions Dad upheld the honour of the society by winning, for them, against visiting clubs. The "Old Wreck" on these auspicious and important events played no small part in our success. Sometimes other members of the society would follow us and drop anchor quite close, and on occasions to the wreck. Later they tried to find answers and explanations why it was that we did so well while they caught so few, not realising that only right on it could the fish be caught.

But our success was our undoing. Murmurs of ill-will grew to out-right bad feeling among a number of members (mostly those who never won anything) and led to an unpleasant and awkward incident. Just before starting in a boat competition two committee members boarded our boat. They apologised for any inconvenience and said that at the request of some of the members, could they examine our boat and baggage etc. It had been suggested that Dad had either caught or bought fish previously to include them in our catch, and it was said that only by this method could we be such consistent winners. They systematically searched our bags, had the floorboards up and checked all likely hiding places but of course found nothing. It was the last thing Dad would have done. He had no need to anyway, unless one counted our secret supply as unfair (a doubt that still troubles me). Satisfied, the searchers reported in our favour and we celebrated the day by winning first and second prizes, which added even more to the ill-feeling of some towards us.

Unable by this means, they sought another way of getting us out of the society. They questioned Dad's "amateur status". When he joined he was engaged in building and decorating but now he had the Beach, digging bait, hiring out boats and even taking fishing parties. Many of them being members themselves of the society, this presented a pretty question. How much of an amateur was he *now*?

The controversy split the committee. Some liked Dad, and apart from that he was a tower of strength for the society against other clubs. He was equally a challenge for the other members to do better. But others wanted him out, we won too often. They argued that he was as near a professional fisherman as made no difference. Dad himself settled it, by offering his resignation. He had no wish to remain where he was not wanted, and his independent nature rebelled against being made a shuttlecock between members, so we left the society.

And with it, I think, a lot of Dad's enthusiasm, because our visits grew less and less to my beloved "Old Wreck", or for that matter fishing at all like we used to.

Then the 1914-18 war came. Fishing, apart from professional fishing, became restricted, and in any case he now spent most of his spare time on his three allotments. And with his sudden and unexpected death in 1917, all visits to the "Old Wreck" ceased for good.

I never went near it again, why I don't know. I still wonder. It was Dad's really. I only shared it when he let me, and when he died I think that privilege seemed to die with him. I knew the marks that pinpointed its position, but never attempted to find it while he was alive. I was content to leave it to him, and had no confidence I could find it, now he was no longer with me. After all I was still only fourteen years old. I doubt I could have even rowed that far in his old dinghy, and even later when I could have done so and searched for it I didn't. I can offer no logical explanation but I shut it right out of my life and in time its very memory faded.

But it was not to be. By some strange chance it was once again, after these many, many, years resurrected and recalled to mind – and I must take the responsibility for inflicting this story on those who are sufficiently interested to read it. The year was now 1981. One hundred years had passed since the "Great Storm" had wreaked its vengeance. Did its rotting timbers, like those of the famous Mary Rose, still lie there? Or had they sunk deep in the sands and no trace remain? I shall never know.

But by a whim of fate one tiny bit of it didn't die, and the story, and those happy, far off days, when I had a passing acquaintance with it, flooded back in memories long lost and forgotten. And in a most unexpected manner.

My cousin's wife, now a widow, after living a lifetime in Leigh, decided her home was far too big, and had the courage to pull up her roots, and buy a little house near her sister in Wanstead. At the bottom of the garden of her home in Leigh was a very large shed, filled with the oddments and collections of nearly eighty years and she generously offered me the choice of anything I would like before disposing of the contents. It was an offer I was unable to resist. Like a child in a toyshop I searched among the shelves and drawers, finding many useful things, and under a pile of rubbish in one corner, a large wooden box. Curiosity made me force the lid and there I found them – encased in straw, a box full of penny clay pipes. My cousin's widow did not know their history. They had been there long before, when my cousin's parents lived there.

But was it just coincidence that his grandfather was chief officer of Customs and Excise during those years of the great storm? On the box the goods were consigned to Deptford, London, and a trade mark looked like "Cornwall". I might be wrong, but I think I know where they came from.

POSTSCRIPT

I have already given two of the marks that when in line give an indication of the position of the "Old Wreck". Unfortunately they are now irrelevant. The crane on the Southend gasworks jetty is no longer there, and owing to the constantly shifting sands the Low Way buoy has been moved a number of times. But a chart of the Thames Estuary around 1910-14 would give the information necessary to anyone interested.

It was also my intention to give the other two marks, but on reflection I decided not to, owing to the fear that some inexperienced or foolhardy person might be tempted to risk their life in an attempt to locate it.

But should any responsible member of an aqua club wish to pursue the matter further, I have left a letter with this extra information in my desk at home.

END